ZOMBIE ECONOMICS

A GUIDE TO PERSONAL FINANCE

LISA DESJARDINS
AND **RICK EMERSON**

ADDITIONAL MATERIAL BY TODD WERKHOVEN

AVERY

Published by the Penguin Group

Penguin Group (USA) Inc., 375 Hudson Street, New York, New York 10014, USA · Penguin Group (Canada), 90 Eglinton Avenue East, Suite 700, Toronto, Ontario M4P 2Y3, Canada (a division of Pearson Penguin Canada Inc.) · Penguin Books Ltd, 80 Strand, London WC2R 0RL, England · Penguin Ireland, 25 St Stephen's Green, Dublin 2, Ireland (a division of Penguin Books Ltd) · Penguin Group (Australia), 250 Camberwell Road, Camberwell, Victoria 3124, Australia (a division of Pearson Australia Group Pty Ltd) · Penguin Books India Pvt Ltd, 11 Community Centre, Panchsheel Park, New Delhi–110 017, India · Penguin Group (NZ), 67 Apollo Drive, Rosedale, North Shore 0632, New Zealand (a division of Pearson New Zealand Ltd) · Penguin Books (South Africa) (Pty) Ltd, 24 Sturdee Avenue, Rosebank, Johannesburg 2196, South Africa

Penguin Books Ltd, Registered Offices: 80 Strand, London WC2R 0RL, Englar.d

Most Avery books are available at special quantity discounts for bulk purchase for sales promotions, premiums, fund-raising, and educational needs. Special books or book excerpts also can be created to fit specific needs. For details, write Penguin Group (USA) Inc. Special Markets, 375 Hudson Street, New York, NY 10014.

Library of Congress Cataloging-in-Publication Data

Desjardins, Lisa.
    Zombie economics : a guide to personal finance / Lisa Desjardins and Rick Emerson ; additional material by Todd Werkhoven.
        p.   cm.
    ISBN 978-1-58333-427-0
    1. Finance, Personal.   I. Emerson, Rick.   II. Werkhoven, Todd.   III. Title.
    HG179.D484   2011   2010048096
    332.024—dc22

Printed in the United States of America
10 9 8 7 6 5 4 3 2 1

BOOK DESIGN BY NICOLE LAROCHE

This publication is designed to provide accurate and authoritative information in regard to the subject matter covered. It is sold with the understanding that the publisher is not engaged in rendering legal, accounting, or other professional services. If you require legal advice or other expert assistance, you should seek the services of a competent professional.

Neither the publisher nor the authors are engaged in rendering professional advice or services to the individual reader. The ideas, procedures, and suggestions contained in this book are not intended as a substitute for consulting with a physician. All matters regarding health require medical supervision. Neither the authors nor the publisher shall be liable or responsible for any loss or damage allegedly arising from any information or suggestion in this book.

While the authors have made every effort to provide accurate telephone numbers and Internet addresses at the time of publication, neither the publisher nor the authors assume any responsibility for errors, or for changes that occur after publication. Further, the publisher does not have any control over and does not assume any responsibility for author or third-party websites or their content.

To Jason.

To Lara.

And to everyone
who is facing down the horde.

Heroes non nascuntur, in angustum locum deprehendentur.

Heroes aren't born, they're cornered.

—T. ABRAM COX

Zom•bie Eco•nom•ics

Noun

1. The theory that every skill needed to survive a financial downturn mirrors a skill needed to survive the zombie apocalypse.
2. A stripped-down, no-nonsense approach to financial survival.

A NOTE FROM THE AUTHORS

This book is not *Secrets to Getting Rich Buying Real Estate,* or *Seven Steps to Winning Big in the Stock Market,* or *Commemorative Coins: Your Gateway to Financial Freedom.* Readers desiring such "solutions" are advised to return this book to its place on the shelf, and perhaps purchase some lottery tickets instead.

CONTENTS

NO ONE IS COMING TO SAVE YOU

AN INTRODUCTION
TO ZOMBIE ECONOMICS

I

t's out there.

On the other side of every door and window, there's a mass of biting, squirming death waiting to pour itself into the house. Day after day, night after night, the clawing and scraping and sickly wet gumming of undead mouths fills the air.

The house is ringed by zombies, and the swarm keeps growing, like flies on wet garbage—too many to fight, too thick to flee.

The moaning is the worst part. It never stops; it just gets louder and louder and attracts more and more zombies.

Little by little, the people inside the house are going insane. From fear, from worry, from the realization that there is no escape.

No one in the house can sleep without screaming, so now, no one sleeps at all.

Instead, they start to count things: the number of potato chip crumbs left inside a bag; the number of water bottles that haven't been drained, cut open, and licked dry; the number of people in a house that seems smaller and more defenseless by the moment.

And the moaning outside keeps getting louder, and the sirens—from somewhere—are blaring, more out of habit than anything else. It's been a long time since there was good news—or any news, for that matter. It's hard to tell if the TV is on some kind of loop, or if there's just nothing to report.

Televisions still *work*, at least—someone, somewhere decided that gods be damned, there would be entertainment until the very end. As humanity smokes and burns and finds itself taken little by little into the mouths of the undead, there will be six thousand channels of nerve-racking nothingness—always the same: "Citizens are advised to monitor this station for updates, and the president has given his assurance that every conceivable measure has been taken to remedy this situation."

Which is the same as yesterday's news. And the day before that, stretching back as far as anyone can recall.

Eventually—tomorrow, perhaps, or next week, or maybe later tonight—the front door, held back by scraps of lumber and whatever nails could be found in the basement, begins to give way. Voices scream for someone to get more nails! Get more nails! But there *are* no more nails. And even if there were, there's no one left to pound them; every shoulder is pressed against the door, holding back a rising tide of the undead, watching as claws come around the edges—filthy, blood-caked hands grasping and scratching. It takes every ounce of strength to keep the door propped up for a few long minutes, and then, there is a flooding sound, like a million noxious sighs all released at once.

And the house is filled.

Gunshots, screams, and gurgled, gnashing gibberish pierce the din . . . then vanish. And what remains are moans, and the sounds of dirty, shuffling feet.

Another home, another family, another future . . . lost.

This will not happen to you.

You will not allow it.

You will survive.

What Is a Zombie Economy?

A Zombie Economy is any financial situation that puts your stability and future in jeopardy. This doesn't necessarily mean a national recession or a collapse of world banking markets (though such things can certainly have consequences for billions of people). A Zombie Economy can be triggered by something as basic as job loss, or by an increase in living costs. It can come from a massive amount of credit card debt or other outstanding loans . . . or it can simply be a series of terrible, unrelated events that combine to destroy your peace of mind. All of these are personal recessions and depressions. *They* are your reality, regardless of how well (or how poorly) things seem to be going in the outside world.

A Zombie Economy can have serious (and sometimes long-term) effects: repossession of your car or other belongings, eviction (or the loss of your home), the inability to pay for college, severely damaged credit, and bankruptcy . . . just to list a few. The repercussions can last for years, even decades.

A Zombie Economy is infectious, contaminating and threatening everything it touches. And, like any infection, it can reach a critical mass, accelerating beyond control. What begins in a single home—or industry, or country—can spread, forming a chain of sickness that endangers thousands . . . or millions.

No one is immune.

A college graduate, saddled with student loans and looking for work, encounters a hiring freeze in her industry; behind on rent and car payments, she finds herself looking for any job available, no matter what it pays.

Married less than a year, a young couple find themselves increasingly arguing about money. As their credit card debt passes $10,000, each accuses the other of overspending, and they begin to consider bankruptcy.

When a traffic accident totals his car and leaves both arms fractured, a freelance carpenter must face three months of unpaid recuperation—along with staggering medical bills and loss of transportation.

In a Zombie Economy, there is a self-perpetuating sense of doom—the feeling that there is *no solution*; that the sickness is unstoppable and the predator unkillable; the fear that even those in command have little idea how to fix things.

Whatever the size of the outbreak, you must protect your **personal economy**.[†] You must confront signs of possible danger before they can do you harm. Do not wait for the infection to announce itself in horrifying, catastrophic ways. Learn to defend yourself in advance—learn to protect your money and your future from the Zombie Economy.

This is not the time to put your faith in others. This is *your* survival at stake, and *you* must make it happen.

No one is coming to save you.

You must save yourself.

IN THE FOLLOWING pages, you will make decisions. You will decide who—and what—to leave behind to ensure your own survival. These decisions will be financial, but may carry emotional consequences. You must think past these challenges and see the larger picture. Think of your own well-being and that of your loved ones and stand by the choices you make, whatever stress or discomfort they may cause. Any such pain is short-term; the end result of doing nothing, however, is ruin—perhaps permanent ruin. A Zombie Economy is dangerous, and, just like the flesh-and-blood variety, it doesn't care who it destroys.

---

† **Personal economy** (*noun*): Your own individual financial situation; the real, day-to-day earnings, losses, and decisions that shape your financial health.

Fortunately, you are *already* armed with a wealth of knowledge for surviving these situations . . . whether you know it or not. This book will help you see your financial issues in terms you will instantly recognize.

Every skill required to survive an economic disaster mirrors a skill required to survive the zombie apocalypse.

Remember that fact at all times, because in your darkest moments, when things seem bleakest, you need to know that there *is* a way out. *There are things you can do.*

Starting now. Starting today.

You will prepare.

You will persevere.

You will adapt.

You will survive.

THROUGHOUT *ZOMBIE ECONOMICS*, you will see three recurring icons, each of which indicates a specific kind of information:

THE BIOHAZARD ICON alerts you to areas of particular danger—situations or actions that pose a greater-than-average threat to your financial stability.

THE HEADSHOT ICON draws your attention to tips, tricks, or strategies—ways to make the most of your finances and to efficiently protect and grow your money.

THE BRAIN FOOD ICON highlights statistics, ideas, analogies, or other information that can aid your understanding and implementation of *Zombie Economics*.

CHAPTER ONE

THE ZOMBIE ON THE BACK PORCH

WHY OPENING THAT PILE OF BILLS WILL SAVE YOUR LIFE

There are zombies in your backyard; of this, you are absolutely sure. The shuffling and the slow scraping sounds are a dead giveaway.

Or an undead giveaway, your brain replies.

But how *many* zombies? That's a different question altogether. For all you know, there could be an *army* of undead creatures gathering outside your house, waiting to pull out your insides like a horrible magic trick.

There's a dull *bump,* followed by an uneven rasping noise—like someone slowly sandpapering the walls.

Could be the wind, you think to yourself.

Or it could be Santa Claus, your brain says. *Or . . . it could be all those zombies who ate the neighbors.*

You're afraid to look through the door's little window for fear of what might be looking back at you. Instead, you pace, and wait, and wonder what might happen if you just never opened that door again.

You've got food (for now), and power (at the moment), and some semblance of protection (you think/pray/hope). The urge to hide upstairs—to get as many doors as possible between you and whatever's waiting outside—is almost overwhelming. *Just for a day or so,* you tell yourself, *just until things calm down—so I can get a plan together.*

You know other people are thinking this way. Hide. Cower. Retreat. Delay. Just for a while.

And you know how all of those people will die. Screaming, running from room to room, still cowering, still retreating. Crazed from hunger and thirst, weakened from days and months of doing nothing, their last weeks on earth spent hiding in a darkened closet, slowly going mad from worry and despair.

No, you decide. Whatever might happen, you will not stand idly by; you will not be a passive spectator to your own horrible demise.

As if waking from a deep, unpleasant dream, you straighten up, inhale, and pull the pistol from your belt.

You walk toward the back door—toward the noise.

This is the shortest chapter in *Zombie Economics,* but it's also the most important. It is the key tenet of surviving the Zombie Economy.

You must open and assess your bills.

Now.

Every one of your bills is a zombie. Every debt, every loan, and every missed payment—they're ghouls, and left alone, they will attract more of their kind. Final notices bring late fees, late fees bring collections, collections bring judgments, and those judgments will destroy your credit, your safety net, and your future.

Equally bad will be the toll on your state of mind. As long as those bills accumulate, stuffed into drawers and stacked into teetering piles of unopened envelopes, your sense of doom and utter hopelessness will only get worse.

Unless you kill them. One by one. Zombie by zombie. Bill by bill.

We don't mean "now" as in "later." We mean "now" as in Now. Right Now. This moment.

There is no time to waste. Every moment those envelopes sit unopened is a moment that drains you of your strength and hope. It's a moment that makes the zombies stronger and makes you weaker.

You will not allow this.

You will fight. And you will do it Now.

THE VERY FIRST STEPS

1. Turn off the television. Turn off the radio. Turn off the phone, the computer, and anything else that makes noise.

2. Set aside a small work space. This should be no bigger than a few square feet and absolutely free of anything else. No decorations, no clutter, no stapler. *Do not buy a desk.* If you don't have a small table, empty out one whole shelf of a bookcase. This is where you will place financial items you are currently using. (Older and/or resolved paperwork, statements, records, etc., should be filed separately.)

3. Open everything—every last piece of mail. Junk, letters, bills, mystery envelopes from Tulsa—all of it.

4. Sort all of the mail into three different categories: junk mail; bills separated by company; personal.

5. Destroy the credit card offers and the junk mail. These are one and the same. Use a shredder if you have one. If you don't have a shredder, you are forbidden to buy one. You'll get one later, as a reward for strong, zombie-killing behavior. Instead, cut up the junk mail and credit card offers. Tiny pieces are best.

6. Place any personal correspondence in a location removed from everything else, such as your nightstand. Remember: This work area is for economic issues only.

7. Take each company's bills and find the most recent for that account. Keep this one, and destroy the others. This will help to avoid confusion, and will ensure that you're dealing with the full amount owed.

8. Set aside the bills dealing with absolute necessities. These are items that allow you to live.

> Think shelter, food, light, water. Think rent, utilities, groceries.*
>
> 9. Pay the "absolute necessities" bills *now*. And by "now," we mean even if it's two o'clock on a Sunday morning. If possible, pay online. Otherwise, write the check, sign the check, seal the envelope, stamp the envelope, and tape it to the front door. (No stamps? You are to go to the nearest open store, buy stamps—three dozen, at least—and proceed with the mailing.)
> 10. We'll wait.

Bam, bam, bam, bam, bam—just like that, you have fewer zombies to deal with, at least for the next thirty days.

Just as important, you've turned your *decision* to survive into *action*. You're no longer just mouthing it, using vague phrases like "I want to save money" or "I'd like to get caught up on my bills"—you've actually *done* something. A crucial step, and one that inevitably leads to the next, and the next, and the next.

You've killed the zombies on the porch.

---

* Also an absolute necessity: anything legally mandated, such as child support, parking tickets, and tax payments. If you drive, consider car insurance as an absolute necessity.

As the final zombie hits the ground, at last made immobile by a shot to the back of its head, you start to wonder, *How did they get into the backyard? Zombies can't climb—why didn't the fence keep them out?*

Heart racing, drenched in sweat, standing in the yard with a nearly empty gun, you scan the perimeter, looking for a hole in the fence. Your eyes stop on the gate . . . which is wide open.

As you secure the swinging metal door, you think, *Gotta weld this shut.*

If only you knew how to weld, your brain replies.

Back inside the house, you slump against a wall. You could sleep for a month. For a year. Forever.

You really ought to do something about that gate, though. You peer at it through one of the bedroom windows.

Windows.

Recoiling, you walk from the bedroom and, standing in the main hallway, turn in a slow circle. You see glass in every direction.

There are windows everywhere.

In the doors, in the walls—every section of the house. Little see-through panes of highly breakable nothing. Your house is covered with them.

And the gate isn't fixed.

Your heart starts pounding.

CHAPTER TWO

FIND ALL THE WEAPONS; BLOCK ALL THE WINDOWS

KNOW YOUR TRUE INCOME . . . AND WHERE IT ACTUALLY GOES

You take a quick survey of the house's contents. You'll be boarding up your windows and doors using whatever you can find lying around. There's no way you're leaving your house until those openings are secured; besides, the nearby stores and lumber yards are probably picked clean—or overrun—by now.

Aware of your rising fatigue, you leave nothing to chance. Clutching a few sheets of paper and a thick, black marker, you walk from room to room, listing each area's weak points. Windows, doors, a window-mounted air conditioner—any place that might allow for easy entry by ghouls (or other humans, for that matter; crises tend to bring out the worst in certain sections of humanity). You double-check your list, knowing that any mistakes might have disastrous consequences later.

Once your tally is complete, you lay out the sheets of paper on the kitchen table.

You have a finite number of supplies: wood, nails, tools— everything must be cobbled together from what is on hand. There's not nearly enough, so you must prioritize.

Windows first, you think, *they're easily breakable.*

You've got a lot of windows, your brain says.

Those closest to the ground, you decide. Zombies can't climb, so anything above ground level can be done later.

Next, that window-mounted air conditioner. You'll hate to lose it, especially since the power is still sporadically working, and God knows how long you'll be stuck here, but that's just a glorified hole in the wall. *One, two, three pushes, and that box will fall inward,* you think, *and after it will come a river of zombies . . . and that, as they say, will be that. It's gotta go.*

Doors. Front door, back door. Can't board those up, either of them. You'll have to leave for supplies eventually, and if something *does* make it through one of the doors, you'll need the other one to get out. You'll brace them, at least. You won't stack anything in front—no sense trapping yourself—but you'll wedge a chair underneath the handle; you can toss it aside if you have to flee. The door hinges are another weak spot, you think, and you make a note to drill deeper screws into the frame when you have a chance.

You take a breath, review your list, and set forth with your hammer—and your pistol.

I n a Zombie Economy, you can easily feel overwhelmed. Stress, confusion, and the constant blaring of the media can conspire to strip you of your confidence and motivation. But you cannot afford this indulgence.

To survive, you must focus and prepare. You want a fortress. But first you must check the walls already in place. This means taking stock of your strengths and, even more important, your weaknesses. You must be aware of your personal situation. That means assessing your real income and your real expenditures.

> You probably don't make what you think, and you probably spend more than you know. These two pieces of misinformation can cripple your finances if not addressed.

This is also a time to discover what you really *owe*. Viewed as a whole, your debt may seem insurmountable, but when taken piece by piece, bill by bill, it becomes a problem to solve—and you'll discover that you *can* solve it.

You will also be amazed at the ease with which you can cut your expenses. Trimming, reducing, and, in many cases, eliminating these financial "weak spots" will be far easier than you ever imagined, but only when you start taking an honest, uncompromising look at your own financial house.

There are decisions to make, and the first one will be made right now: you must set aside the time to make this chapter work. That means reclaiming valuable hours from the television, the Internet, and whatever else might keep you in a state of fear-stricken inaction—your head full of anxiety and stress, with no end in sight and no remedy at hand. The remedy is within reach, but only if you pursue it seriously.

Take a moment, make the decision to live, and turn the page.

This chapter is about identifying your surroundings, your resources, and your weak spots. You must know every nook, cranny, and cubbyhole; any place that might pose a threat . . . or serve as sanctuary. Only then can you begin securing your financial house.

You will accomplish this in three steps:

ONE: Identify your actual income.

TWO: Determine if you are overpaying the government in every paycheck.

THREE: Learn how you really spend your money—and where you can stop the leaks.

To survive a Zombie Economy, you must know every aspect of your own financial situation—your assets *and* your limitations.

That starts with determining your actual take-home income. Most of us *think* we know how much we make, but the difference between that figure and reality can be surprising . . . even shocking. Start now, with the worksheet on the next page.

STEP 1: Identifying your actual income

WORKSHEET #1: YOUR ACTUAL, PRIMARY INCOME

1. FIRST

Write the dates and amounts of your last six paychecks.

If you earn the same amount with every paycheck, skip to "3. NEXT" and write down that amount as the average.

Date   **Paycheck Amount**
                            (after taxes, health care, all deductions)

_____   _____

_____   _____

_____   _____

_____   _____

_____   _____

_____   _____

PAYCHECK TOTAL: _____

Not sure about the amounts? Check your bank records or ask your employer. If there is a Human Resources department or website, that is the first place to check. If not, contact your company's business office.

Note: If you are self-employed, estimate the amount that you were paid by clients for each of the past six months (or as close to six months as possible). You can calculate this figure using your bank account and check deposits.

If you earn money from tips, see Worksheet #2.

2. NEXT

Determine your Average Paycheck. It's simple math, laid out simply . . .
so there are no excuses for skipping this.

_____ ÷ 6 = _____
Paycheck total above   Avg. Paycheck

3. NEXT

Determine your Average Monthly Income—what you actually take
home in a typical month. Fill out the *one* line below that applies to you.

If you're paid once a month:

_____ = _____
Avg. Paycheck from above   Monthly Paycheck Avg. [CIRCLE AMOUNT]

If you're paid twice a month:*

_____ x 2 = _____
Avg. Paycheck from above   Monthly Paycheck Avg. [CIRCLE AMOUNT]

If you're paid every week:

_____ x 4 = _____
Avg. Paycheck from above   Monthly Paycheck Avg. [CIRCLE AMOUNT]*

---

* Yes, we know, many months have five weeks. In *Zombie Economics*, you never overestimate
your strength; you *build* your strength. Here, by coming up with the minimum or lowest income average, you are giving yourself a cushion during those months when you *do* get five
weeks and another paycheck.

4. NEXT

Does the result (your Average Monthly Income) seem correct to you? If not, check your math. Then double-check your math. If the figure remains the same, you must accept that this is what you make for one month's work.

THE END

Monthly Paychecks, on average = _____

Put circled figure from #3 here and circle it again.

NOW, go to Worksheet #3, unless you also make money from tips.

WORKSHEET #2: WHAT YOU REALLY MAKE IN TIPS

Tips are like air ducts: out of sight, but a very real factor in your home's safety. To obtain a truly complete picture of your structure's preparedness, you must take such seemingly small variables into account.

This slice of income can be maddeningly difficult to quantify, but chaotic times call for redoubled effort, and this area of your income is no exception. Remember: Vigilance in all areas is necessary if you are to outlast the undead menace.

1. FIRST

Fill out this form over the next two weeks. (Hint: Repeat this often. Tip income changes frequently.)

Date	Take-Home Tips
_____	_____
_____	_____
_____	_____

_____   _____
_____   _____
_____   _____
_____   _____
_____   _____
_____   _____
_____   _____
_____   _____
_____   _____

TWO-WEEK TOTAL: _____
(Add all entries from above)

2. NEXT
Figure out your monthly tip average.

_____ x 2 = _____
Two-week total above   Monthly Tips on Avg.

THE END
Monthly Tips (avg.) = _____
Write that figure again. [CIRCLE AMOUNT]

HINT: You should keep track of your tips regularly—at least every other month. They can fluctuate wildly due to circumstances beyond your control. It's also worth asking: Is any one factor affecting your tips (a particular shift, particular route, or a particular section)? If so, can you replicate these high-tipping conditions as much as possible? See ZombieEconomics.com for a chart that makes tracking tip conditions easier.

You are facing the zombie horde, so you must take stock of every potential weapon, no matter how small. From pistols to pitchforks, everything must be assessed.

So it is with your income. You must make sure you are considering every bit of your financial power. It is your obligation if you are to outlast the Zombie Economy.

This could include freelance work, revenue from investments, or odd jobs. This income must be accounted for—and deposited in your bank account before a single dollar can escape.

1. FIRST

List any regular income that is separate from your primary paycheck. Give your best guess, then figure out weekly averages.

Income Source	Amount Every X Weeks	Weekly Avg. *(Divide Amount by X)*
Ex: *House Painting $300*	*every 6 weeks*	*$50* ($300 ÷ 6)*
_____	_____	_____
_____	_____	_____
_____	_____	_____
_____	_____	_____
_____	_____	_____
_____	_____	_____
_____	_____	_____
_____	_____	_____

---

* The number by which you divide comes from column 3 and is the number of weeks between payments for this job. If you get paid every week, the number would be 1.

_____ _____ _____

_____ _____ _____

_____ _____ _____

TOTAL OF WEEKLY AVERAGES: _____

2. NEXT

Convert your Total Weekly Average into a monthly number.*

_____ x 4 = _____

Total Weekly Avgs. (above)   Other income you make each month,

on average

THE END

Other monthly income (avg.) = _____

Write the figure from above. [CIRCLE AMOUNT]

_____

* Yes, we could have just asked for monthly estimates. But this method is more likely to be accurate.

WORKSHEET #4: INCOME SUMMARY SHEET

When in doubt, this is where you look to see your actual, real-life income. To know it. To be able to protect it.

1. FIRST
Enter the circled numbers from the past three worksheets here.

MONTHLY PAYCHECKS (Avg.): _____

MONTHLY TIPS (Avg.): _____

MONTHLY OTHER INCOME (Avg.): _____

2. NEXT
Add them up. Write below.

THE END
MONTHLY INCOME (Avg.): _____
[CIRCLE AMOUNT]

ONE LAST THING
Go to the back of this book, to the "Key Survival Numbers" page. Write the above number (Monthly Income) in the appropriate space.

You've just taken a major step forward in Zombie Economics—and overcome a challenge that dooms the less determined. But there are bigger dangers ahead, and the path to safety is not always clear.

It's time to talk about taxes and withholding.

As with so many elements of Zombie Economics, you understand more about taxes and withholding than you might first realize.

Think of it this way:

When zombies swarm through your city, you see terrified humans engaging in any behavior they think might spare their lives. Nothing is more common—or futile—than attempts to distract the creatures with traditional food. Over and over, you see it played out: man is besieged by the living dead, man frantically throws his supplies and provisions at this writhing, moaning horde, who, of course, steadily advance on the poor human, who now finds himself just as surrounded, but without his food . . . food he must attempt to reclaim later, once (and if) the zombies disperse.

Tax **Withholdings**[†] operate the same way. When you withhold too much, you are, in essence, overpaying your taxes, and throwing extra money at the government . . . money that you *will* get back later, but without interest, without a bonus, and without any sort of benefit.

While it is tempting to view a tax refund as a good thing, you have actually *lost* money in the process. You have, in effect, given the government a free loan and, in the meantime, deprived yourself of interest that is rightfully yours.

---

† **Withholding** (*noun*): (1) Monies automatically taken from your paycheck and applied to anticipated yearly taxes. (2) Something that many overpay.

Are you withholding too much? Let's find out. There's a simple way, and a longer (but more thorough) way. Let's start by getting some facts down on paper. Head directly to the next worksheet.

WORKSHEET #5: INCOME WITHHOLDING

1. FIRST*

Obtain a copy of your W-4—this is the tax form your employer must file with the IRS. Ask your supervisor or Human Resources department for a copy.

2. NEXT

Now, look at line 5 of your W-4: "Total Allowances You Are Claiming." Write that number below.

ALLOWANCES You Claim: _____

3. NEXT

Determine your dependents. Respond to each line as appropriate.

____ You. Enter "1" to declare that you are, in fact, dependent on yourself. Almost everyone enters "1" here.

____ Spouse. Enter "1" if you have a nonworking spouse or domestic partner.

---

* If your parents claim you as a dependent, skip this worksheet and discuss your withholding with them.

____ Children. Enter the number of children you claim as "dependent" on you.

____ Elderly parents. Enter the number living with/financially depending on you.

____ Others. Enter the number of other people who rely on you to pay the vast majority of their expenses. (Usually, this means they live in your home. This is also relatively rare. If you aren't sure, check the IRS.gov website for more info.)

_____ TOTAL Dependents. (Add the numbers immediately above.)

4. NEXT

Gauge if you're withholding the right amount by answering these questions:

Is the number of your total dependents larger than
   the allowances on your W-4? _____
Do you get a sizable tax refund every year? _____
Do you expect a tax refund next year? _____

If you answered "yes" to two or more of these, you may be withholding too much from your paychecks.

OPTION

If you'd like to take a more thorough look at the issue of your withholdings, and make a more in-depth assessment, go to http://www.irs.gov, and in the search window type in "withholding calculator." This will give you a link to the IRS's web-based withholding calculator; go through it to determine what you should be withholding on your W-4.

5. NEXT

If appropriate, change your withholding. Ask your employer to turn in a new W-4 for you, one reflecting the new number of exemptions (the number of broad deductions the IRS gives you, including one for yourself and one for each dependent). You can do this at any time.

6. NEXT

Watch.

If you raise the number of your exemptions, you should see the size of your paycheck increase (though it could take several weeks for this to take effect). If, after four weeks, your paycheck amount remains unchanged, contact your Human Resources director and have them follow up.

THE END

Above all, be sure to ask questions of your employer/HR department as you analyze—and possibly adjust—your withholdings. Even if you're confident that you know the answers, it never hurts to have clarification or a second opinion—especially when your money's at stake.

STEP 2: Assessing your cost of living— and what's left over

In chapter 2, you opened your existing bills and identified the absolute necessities (rent/mortgage, utilities, transportation, credit card minimum payments, government-mandated payments).

It's time to find out what these necessities are costing you and how much money you have left for additional expenses.

WORKSHEET #6: ABSOLUTE NECESSITIES AND YOUR OPERATING FUND

In a world overrun by zombies, every decision becomes a calculation: How badly do I need to leave the house today? How much do I need to eat to maintain my health? With God-knows-what possibly lumbering down my street, do I dare leave the lights on?

In a Zombie Economy, every decision must be considered a crucial one. There are no "incidentals" and nothing is "disposable."

It's time to take a cold, hard look at what you need to survive and what you don't. This is not a time for self-deception; this is a time for honesty—with yourself, about your present, and for your future.

1. FIRST

Pin down your current absolute necessities. Pull out the bills you set aside earlier, look at your bank records (what you've paid out in the past), and fill in the chart below. Take your time (more than one sitting if you need) to get it right.

Expense

Monthly Cost
(round up to nearest dollar)

SHELTER

Mortgage _____

Rent _____

Electric _____

Gas (heat, etc.) _____

Water _____

Condo or Homeowners Fee _____
(if not included above)

COMMUNICATIONS

Phone/Internet _____

TRANSPORTATION

Car Payment or Motorcycle, etc.   _____

Car Insurance   _____

Gasoline   _____

Mass Transit   _____

OBLIGATIONS

Student Loans   _____

Minimum Credit
Card payments (all cards)   _____

Alimony   _____

FAMILY

Child Care   _____

Diapers/Baby Food   _____

Child Support   _____

School Tuition   _____

Pet Food/Care   _____

HEALTH

Medicine/Prescriptions   _____

Health Insurance Premium   _____

Enter only if you pay this outside of work
(if it is not automatically deducted from your paycheck).

FOOD

Your Best Guess Will Do   _____

Remember: We're talking about necessities: the minimum you need to get by.

Later, we'll talk about expanding on that.

OTHER

_____   _____

_____   _____
_____   _____
_____   _____
_____   _____
_____   _____
_____   _____

2. NEXT

Total all of those monthly necessities up. Write that figure below.

Absolute Necessities (monthly): _____

CIRCLE AMOUNT and add to list at end of the book.

THE END

Go back to Worksheet #4 (page 27) and find your Average Monthly Income. Write below. Then copy the absolute necessities figure from above, and subtract.

     Average Income: _____

- Absolute Necessities: _____

= MONTHLY OPERATING FUND:_____

CIRCLE AMOUNT and add to list at end of the book.

NOTE: In Zombie Economics, the difference between your income and your absolute necessities is your Operating Fund. It is not "leftover money" or "pocket money," and above all, it is not to be called **Disposable Income.**[†]

[†] **Disposable Income** (*noun*): (1) Insidious, destructive term created by those who wish for your money to become theirs. (2) A term that, when used in conversation, may indicate that the user has become infected.

STEP 3: Assessing your cost of living—and what's left over

You have barricaded your doors and lower windows. Now it's time to seal off the upper windows, damaged walls, and any other openings in your financial house.

This is, once again, a time for honesty. Where are your financial weak spots?

Using the next worksheet, make a list of your nonnecessary expenses. Pinpoint the myriad costs that can be decreased or eliminated: gym memberships, late fees, game rentals, restaurants—you name it.

You must be honest; anything less will leave multiple openings into your financial home . . . tiny broken windows everywhere.

1. FIRST

Make a truthful estimate of what you spend each month on things that are *not* absolute necessities. We've given you some general categories, as well as room to add your own. Put down all amounts, no matter how small.

Note: Ignore the third column, "Monthly Goal," for now.

Expense	Monthly Spending Now	Monthly Goal
ENTERTAINMENT		
Cable/Satellite TV	_____	_____
Pay-Per-View Movies/Events	_____	_____
Movie Rental or Other Late Fees	_____	_____
Online Gaming	_____	_____
Magazine/Newspaper Subscriptions	_____	_____
Concerts/Sports	_____	_____
Other	_____	_____
Other	_____	_____
HOME & HEALTH		
Gym Membership	_____	_____
Hair/Salon Expenses	_____	_____
Dry Cleaning	_____	_____
Landscaping or Cleaning Companies	_____	_____
Incompleted Home Projects	_____	_____
Other	_____	_____

Expense	Monthly Spending Now	Monthly Goal
Other	_____	_____
Other	_____	_____

FOOD

Food—Delivered	_____	_____
Food—In Restaurant	_____	_____
Food—In Bar	_____	_____
Coffee/Coffee Drinks (outside home)	_____	_____
Groceries at Convenience Stores	_____	_____
Groceries at Upscale/Gourmet Stores	_____	_____
Groceries purchased but not used before expiration	_____	_____
Other	_____	_____
Other	_____	_____
Other	_____	_____

VICES

Cigarettes/Tobacco	_____	_____
Alcohol	_____	_____
Other Intoxicants	_____	_____
Other	_____	_____
Other	_____	_____
Other	_____	_____

OTHER POTENTIAL DANGERS

Unnecessary Clothing Purchases	_____	_____
Electronics/Gadgets	_____	_____

Expense	Monthly Spending Now	Monthly Goal
Software/Apps/Upgrades/ Website Subscriptions	_____	_____
Other	_____	_____
Other	_____	_____
Other	_____	_____
Other	_____	_____
Other	_____	_____
Other	_____	_____
Other	_____	_____
Other	_____	_____
Other	_____	_____
Other	_____	_____
Other	_____	_____
Other	_____	_____

2. NEXT

Total up all the above. Write the tally below.

Potential Monthly Leaks _____ CIRCLE THIS;
add to Key Survival Numbers in back of book.

3. NEXT

As you've probably guessed, the next step is to lower these expenses. Not randomly, not sporadically, but with tangible, concrete objectives. Use the third column to list your goal—the amount to which you will reduce your spending on each item. Try to get as close to $0 as possible without inflicting abject suffering upon yourself.*

---

* Strong preliminary goals include: totally eliminating one out of every four non–absolute necessities expenses, and reducing the total monthly non–absolute necessities outgoing amount by 50 percent.

THE END

As your *Zombie Economics* skills become sharper, you will naturally revisit this page; your goals will become stronger; your expenses will be leaner and more controlled. If this page gets messy, go to Zombie Economics.com for a brand-new copy, ready for the using.

WHEN YOU HAVE created your list of nonnecessary expenses, look for ways to reduce or eliminate these costs. Some will seem obvious; many, less so:

- Your current television package—How many of your available channels do you actually watch? Of the channels you do watch, are those programs available elsewhere (DVD, online, etc.)? If you already have a high-speed Internet connection, this could obviate or reduce many of your other media expenses.
- Your current cell phone plan—What features are you paying for? What features are you actually using? Assess your minutes, your texting options, e-mail options, etc. Determine what you use, what you don't use, and—most important—what you actually need, and scale down your service accordingly.*
- Movie/video game rentals—If you currently rent movies and/or video games from a retail outlet, how much are you paying in late fees? Consider using a subscription service, which, while adding a monthly expenditure, would eliminate

---

* Such costs (most costs, in fact) are usually negotiable. Though we're trained to pay what the sticker or price tag says, nearly everything can be reduced by the mere process of asking. This is especially true when dealing with a company that wishes to keep you as a customer. Cable companies, cell phone providers, fitness centers, and numerous other businesses are usually more than willing to reduce your costs or adjust your plan if it means keeping you out of a competitor's clutches. The first step? Simply tell them you'd like to cancel your service. You'll be amazed at how quickly they come around. Remember: The Zombie Economy is hurting *them,* too.

your late fees altogether. If you already utilize a subscription-based service, assess whether you are getting your money's worth. Many such services have a tiered system, offering a set amount of rentals at a time—or per month—for a flat monthly fee; the higher the fee, the higher the number of simultaneous rentals/downloads.

- Books/magazines/newspapers—Though many (if not most) newspapers and magazines make their content freely available online, the library remains an underused financial resource. With the cost of hardcover books hovering somewhere between "exorbitant" and "insane," the library is an invaluable portal to an infinite number of books. Zombie Economics means having a library card . . . and using it.
- Shopping at warehouse clubs—Examine your costs: Do you save more than the price of your membership?
- Insurance—Look into the details of your insurance plans. You might be paying for more than you think. Automotive insurance can be especially costly, often because of added elements you simply don't need. Discuss your insurance needs with your company or agent. Do you need full coverage? Liability? Do areas in your insurance plans overlap, and can some of this overlap be eliminated? Don't hesitate to get a second opinion, and don't hesitate to shop around. Your patronage is valuable, and many times businesses will offer you a better deal in hopes of making you a long-term customer.

Zombie Economics require honesty in self-assessment. You must determine your absolute necessities, and you must start reducing (or eliminating) everything else. You will find, in most cases, that you never miss what you once thought you couldn't live without. Your house will be stronger. You will be stronger.

You know this. Zombie Economics mean acting.

Don't Feed Them, It Only Encourages Them: Eliminating Your Credit Card Problem, Once and for All

Since their creation in 1950, credit cards have spread debt to every corner of the globe. Their misuse creates a choking web of financial disease that, all too often, attracts other lenders and accelerates the problem, with each wave of fresh credit offers further crippling your fiscal stability. Credit cards are the Zombie Economy incarnate.

When you face credit card debts (and their accompanying interest rates), it's impossible not to feel overwhelmed—caught in the cold, clutching hands of red ink and minimum monthly payments.

So complete and total is the intermingling between credit cards and financial strife that we have set aside this special section specifically for the purpose of dealing with your credit card debt. Here, you will determine which of your cards need immediate attention—which pose the gravest danger—and you will learn the fastest, most effective way of paying down your debt.

You will not, however, learn about quick-relief schemes, magical plans that eliminate your credit card bills overnight, or any other such nonsense. A Zombie Economy requires honesty and total commitment to changing your financial behavior.

If you *cannot* completely pay off your credit card bills each month, you should be paying at least the monthly minimum for every single credit card on which you owe a balance. To do otherwise means penalties and late fees, and is no better than burning your money in the backyard barbecue.

You will, however, give *one* of your credit cards extra attention (and extra money). To assess which card, do the following:

Find out the annual percentage rate (APR) for each of your cards. This is sometimes referred to simply as "the interest rate." You will find this information on each card's monthly bill. If you don't have a bill for a given card, you can find out the APR by calling the customer service number printed on the back of the card.

WORKSHEET #8: NAMING YOUR ENEMY: YOUR CREDIT CARD BILLS

1. FIRST
List each card or debt that you owe, followed by the APR.

This list should also include things being paid on an installment plan: furniture, electronics, etc.; these are fundamentally the same as credit cards. Student loans should be included on this list, but should be ranked at the absolute bottom, under all other cards and payments, because student-loan payments are tax-deductible.

Credit Card or Debt Name   **APR %**

THE END

Figure out the ranks. Looking at the APRs above, write your debts in order, so that the highest APR is on top. *Paying this is your first priority.*

Rank	Credit Card or Debt Name	APR %
____	_____	_____
____	_____	_____
____	_____	_____
____	_____	_____
____	_____	_____
____	_____	_____
____	_____	_____
____	_____	_____
____	_____	_____
____	_____	_____
____	_____	_____
____	_____	_____

You are now armed with two crucial pieces of information:

1. Your remaining monthly income after absolute necessities have been paid;
2. The list of credit cards on which you owe money and their priority ranking by APR.

Each month, beginning now, you will pay off as much of your highest-priority card as possible. Other cards can be given the bare minimum—enough to avoid late or penalty fees—but the highest-priority card must be given your full financial attention. Every month. Without fail. Period.

This is as nonnegotiable as paying for electricity or rent. You will put money toward this card the minute your absolute necessities are paid. You will contribute as much as you possibly can toward resolving this card's debt. You will do this every single month, without fail. No exceptions. Ever.

Example:

You have a $1,000 balance on credit card X, which carries an 18 percent APR.

Typically, your minimum monthly payment would be 4 percent of the balance, meaning you are only expected to pay $40 a month. If you follow this method of payment, it will take you roughly two years, eight months, and an extra $264 to pay this off. A $1,000 purchase will cost you $1,264.

However, if you simply doubled your monthly payment (from $40 to $80), it would reduce the life of the debt by more than half, so it would now take you just fourteen months and an extra $117 to pay off this debt. You have stopped yourself from handing the credit card company nearly $150 extra.

Once your highest-priority card is completely paid down, it's time to start killing off the rest. Referring to your list of the cards and their APRs, move to the card with the second-highest interest rate. Repeat the process you used with card number one—but now, take the amount you were paying every month for card number one (which was far above the minimum, since that card was your highest priority) and apply that to card number two . . . on top of card number two's minimum monthly payments. Pay this combined amount every month, without fail, until card number two is completely free and clear.

You are killing zombies one by one. You are getting stronger.

Continue this process, working your way down the list of credit cards/payments. As you pay off each card, you will not only be freed from its minimum monthly payment, but you will have more money to shoot down the next card on the list. You'll be able to wipe out each card more quickly than the one before it.

You are now addressing what you owe.

Of equal importance is this vow to yourself: For as long as you are paying off your debts, you will absolutely not put one single dollar on credit. No cards, no installments, no rent-to-own.

You are clawing your way out of a hole; there is no reason to make it any deeper. Stop digging your own grave.

YOU'VE COMPLETED ONE of the most crucial steps in Zombie Economics: you've fortified your financial structure. It's just as important to examine and refine your plan as time goes on. Such fine-tunings are a positive step; they show that you are learning and following your own financial behavior more closely. Did you cut back on your movie subscription plan, only to realize that you had used that service far more often than cable television? Make the adjustment.

Set reminders to study your plan and current situation. These can be put in your day planner, on a calendar kept with your other financial materials, or into one of the many free online schedule/alert services. Set weekly, monthly, and yearly reminders, each of them referring you to a list of specific items to review. Remember: Your plan will work only if you follow it.

It is crucial that your process be ongoing. Only by boarding up the windows, bracing every door, and strengthening every weak point will you make it through the Zombie Economy.

Your success will not be measured in bright, shiny objects. Your success will be measured by survival.

You never thought you'd be boarding up the *outside* of a window.

With a series of hammer bangs, you finish, and step back.

The house's exterior is covered in pieces of old furniture, bookcase shelves, broom handles, and random bits of wood found inside the attic.

The interior of the house was done more cleanly—you took your time there, sort of—but once every single opening was covered from the inside, you started thinking: *They can't climb. That means they don't have any kind of motor skills . . . not good ones, anyway.*

If that's true, your brain replies, *then—*

Five minutes later, you are outside, using your leftover nails and wood to cover the exteriors. *If they can't climb, they probably can't pull,* you think, *and even if they can, this still gives me twice the time to figure something out. Twice as much protection . . . why not?*

It isn't smooth sailing. You kill one zombie while working outside, and you are positive you hear another, even though you can't find it.

Working as fast as safety allows, you focus on the job at hand. Now, surveying the house, you nod to yourself, thinking, *It'll work.*

And then you hear it.

Where is it? Where the hell is it? You whirl, looking for the source of the noise.

The ground, says your brain, *check the ground.*

Jesus.

The zombie has lost its legs—somewhere. It is crawling through a section of tall, uncut grass—not dead, not alive, mouth snapping and gurgling.

Well, okay, your brain says, *they can pull a little bit.*

You stumble back, pulling the pistol from your makeshift tool belt.

Aim.

Fire.

The gun clicks; nothing happens.

For the love of—

In a flash, you're in the house, throwing the door shut behind you and rummaging for more ammunition. You never, ever had any idea you'd need so many bullets all at once.

Your fingers find a box of ammunition in the back of your utility closet. Loading the pistol as you walk, you exit the back door, find the crippled ghoul, and kill it with two shots to the head.

A quick look around, and then you're back inside your home, reloading the gun, and wondering where you can get more bullets.

CHAPTER THREE

A BASEMENT
FULL OF AMMO

SAVE YOURSELF BY SAVING MONEY

Let us now give thanks, you think, before blasting open the door of someone's vacant house, *for the great American shotgun.* Created in 1878 by Daniel LeFever, the shotgun is the Swiss army knife of firearms: part truncheon, part zombie killer, part burglar repellent . . . and one-size-fits-all picker of locks.

Boom.

The door seems to explode backward in its frame, slamming open on its hinges and giving you an unrestricted view of the living room.

Stepping through a mist of debris, you take your first cautious steps past the threshold. Things that appear abandoned and empty sometimes aren't, you've learned. All too often, a family will board themselves up in their home, never knowing until it's too late that one of them is infected. Months later, when *you* come by, searching for supplies, the house seems quiet and still—it's only once you're inside that you hear the rattling moans.

You move sideways into the kitchen, keeping your breathing steady and quiet. You open one drawer at a time, then the cupboards, then move down the hallway to a closet at the far end.

You've been doing this for about six weeks now—ever since your encounter with the crawling ghoul in the backyard. First, you upgraded your gun. At a massive, pawnshop-style store a few miles away, the shelves had been picked clean, but no one had bothered to check behind the counter. There, tucked away underneath the register, was a single-barreled 12-gauge—probably meant for use against stickup artists. Now, it's part of your anti-zombie arsenal.

At the end of the hallway, you open the closet door, and your left hand immediately goes to the top shelf. You rummage by touch, feeling for cardboard, metal, or boxes of any kind.

You're looking for ammunition.

A shotgun is, by itself, fundamentally useless—little more than a club with a pretty handle.

So you look for ammunition. *Always and first.*

And you take all the ammo you find. *Always and first.* Water, food, nails, or other supplies come a distant second.

You take the ammo first. No matter how much you already have. No matter how heavy your backpack becomes. No matter how long the walk back home.

And use it only when you have to.

You don't use it to hunt. You don't use it for practice. You don't use it to signal. You don't use it for anything but survival . . . and when searching for more ammunition.

Take it.

Store it.

Save it.

Repeat.

Survive.

n Zombie Economics, your savings—your money in the bank—is your ammunition stockpile, and you must grow it and guard it with every ounce of energy you possess.

Automotive issues, sudden medical expenses, rental or mortgage crises—these things can come from nowhere and appear on your figurative doorstep, pounding and groaning and threatening your safety. With a well-stocked financial arsenal, you can blast them into nothingness. With an empty savings account, you're standing there, defenseless, wondering how long the door will hold . . . waiting for the moment when it finally splinters.

Savings is key, and increasing it is your number-one priority— every paycheck, every month, without fail . . . even if you never use it.

And you shouldn't.

We cannot stress this point often enough or loudly enough: your savings is like a fire extinguisher or your vehicle's air bag—you hope to never use them, but by God, you want them tested and ready if that moment ever comes.

And make no mistake—cash can be a lifesaver, especially in a Zombie Economy. When financial times are tough, cash carries weight that credit just can't match. Purchases that *seem* nonnegotiable (on credit) become infinitely more flexible once real dollars are on the table. Cash will buy you out of situations in ways that nothing else can. For this reason alone, money in the bank—never under your mattress, never in a coffee can out back—also gives you a psychological advantage: the knowledge that whatever happens, you are prepared. You have the ammunition.

Take, store, save, repeat—starting with the minimum: a savings account.

YOU'VE HEARD IT a million times: pay yourself first.

This is, of course, boring.

We're not going to argue the point. There's nothing especially thrilling about putting money in the bank . . . until you need it and it's not there. Then your life becomes all *kinds* of exciting. The evicted kind. The sleeping-on-a-friend's-sofa-for-three-months kind. The taking-the-bus-twenty-five-miles-to-interview-for-a-job-you-probably-won't-get kind. The asking-your-parents-to-pay-your-bills kind. The moving-back-home kind.

Excitement is overrated.

The point is that your security and your ability to avoid everything we've mentioned above depend on *you*. No one is going to do this for you. And no pair of $150 sunglasses will keep your car from being repossessed. You can't pay your collection agent with a cell phone. A designer scarf will not keep a zombie from ripping out your voice box.

Only a fully loaded gun—and truckloads of ammo—will protect you from that.

The first step to building your savings stockpile: pay yourself 10 percent before you pay anyone else.* That 10 percent needs to be as real as the taxes taken out of your paycheck. It is not an option. That money goes right into your savings. Every paycheck, every time. If you do not commit to saving this 10 percent *every* time you get paid, it will become sporadic, and "sporadic" inevitably becomes "never." You will find reason after reason not to do it. Get rid of those excuses this instant. You are in survival mode.

---

* Yes, that means *before* paying such things as credit card bills. The relative downside of owing additional interest on these debts pales in comparison to the dangers of having no savings.

Bullets Beget Bullets

When it comes to savings, compounding is everything. Without it, your interest is just a few pennies on the dollar—still pennies worth saving, but nothing to write home about. **Compounded Interest**[†]— which is offered everywhere—makes your money multiply itself repeatedly, turning your savings into a machine that generates its own income. Though the amounts will initially be meager, they will increase exponentially over time, with the true beauty being this: every cent of that increase, no matter how sizable, is given to you by the bank—simply *handed to you* as your reward for being a responsible, upright **Zombie Economist**.[††]

Here's how it works:

Suppose your net income is $30,000 a year. Banking 10 percent of that wage (paying yourself first) means you put $3,000 in savings—itself worthy of congratulations. If your savings account offers a 3 percent return, you'll earn $90 in interest that first year.[*]

The following year (assuming you don't get a raise, and still bring home $30,000), banking another 10 percent brings your total savings deposit to $6,000, but now you're adding in the $90 interest the bank paid you last year, for a grand total of $6,090. Interest on *that* is $182.70.

[†] **Compounded Interest** (*noun*): A situation in which interest is added to the principal/initial amount; from that moment on, the interest that has been added itself also earns interest.

[††] **Zombie Economist** (*noun*): One who operates according to the principles of Zombie Economics. Is not synonymous with "wealthy," as Zombie Economics is a behavior system applicable to any stage of your financial development.

[*] Should anyone be tempted to dismiss the idea of compounded interest at this early stage, consider a couple of things:
   (a) That $90 is money that you earned on the money you invested last time around. You didn't paint a house for it; you didn't flip burgers for it—you got it because your money is already starting to replicate itself.
   (b) You didn't think we'd go to all this trouble to get you a measly $90, did you? We don't steer you wrong; keep reading.

The most impressive thing in the above example is the interest, or amount of money the bank is giving you every year. This is the amount of money the bank is actually *giving* you every year. And every single year, that number will increase—money you earn by doing absolutely nothing.

Take, store, save, repeat.

Always.

Another reason to build your savings: banks, business lenders, and other financial institutions use a number of factors when determining your worthiness (or lack thereof) for loans, credit lines, lowered interest rates, etc.

A well-managed savings account goes a long way toward demonstrating the willpower and good judgment that these folks look for; this will be critical if, for example, you need to take out a home loan or start your own company.

And, as we all know from grade school, money in the bank builds interest on itself. The bottom line is it's free money being offered to you, and all you have to do in return is . . . nothing. Bullets are bullets.

If setting aside 10 percent out of every single paycheck seems a bit overwhelming, think about it this way: if your boss informed you, tomorrow, that all salaries, company-wide, were being cut by 10 percent, would you survive? Of course you would. You'd complain, and curse, and lament the shoddy state of affairs, but you'd get by. You always do. And this is no different.

So for you, starting now, that 10 percent doesn't exist. Period. It's gone, gone before you ever see it. It's in the basement with all the other ammo, gathering dust and waiting for an onslaught, which, hopefully, will never come—which leads us to the single biggest reason that your savings must come first: **You never know when a Zombie Economy will appear**. Unemployment, illness, a sudden automotive or housing emergency—the list of dangers lurking Out There is nearly endless, and when Out There is at your front door, you'll thank God and good judgment for that basement full of ammo. *Your savings will save you—* it will give you time, options, and the freedom to not panic. But *it* can't do *its* job until *you* do *yours*.

Right about now, your brain is compiling a list of excuses why you can't put away that 10 percent. Do any of these sound familiar?

Q: Shouldn't I be paying off my credit cards first?
A: Credit cards are insidious, and add significant amounts of mental stress. That said, addressing your credit card debt (and keeping it from recurring) requires a certain brand of self-discipline, and saving that 10 percent is real, tangible proof of your financial strength and willpower. When you can put 10 percent in the bank without blinking, without hesitating, you will look in the mirror and, little by little, see someone else. As part of that, you'll view credit cards—and debt in general—much differently.

On a more basic level, if you have significant amounts of credit card debt, much of the damage is already done. While we are not diminishing the importance of paying what you owe, a lack of savings poses a much more serious threat than additional interest tacked onto an already existing credit card bill.

Q: I'm completely broke. Shouldn't I recover a little before I start putting away that much of my income?

A: Are you *completely* broke? As in destitute? As in living in your car? In a shelter? At home with your parents? (If you answered "living with my parents," the folks in the shelter would like a word with you regarding "destitution.")

Quite simply, if you're not homeless and you're not starving, you are not destitute, period. This is no time to underestimate the gravity of your situation, but you will get nowhere by *overstating* the case. Remember, absolute necessities are called that for a reason, and anything that doesn't fit the category is off the menu until your finances are stable.

Q: I'm going to school/going back to school. Shouldn't that be my priority?

A: Going to school—any school, be it college, trade lessons, or night classes to nail down your GED—is admirable and valuable. Your devotion to education will pay off, and doors will open with less effort because of it . . . someday. Right now, you need to secure your fiscal situation, because a partial degree won't fix your car, buy your groceries, or keep you off the streets if your rent goes up. By choosing to further your education, you have demonstrated a greater degree of motivation than is possessed by *many* people; now, it's time to prove yourself better than *most* people.

Save, scrimp, and study. In that order.

Take, store, save, repeat . . . *and do not touch that money.* Act like it's not even there. Do not use it for a special treat. Do not use it for a one-off expense. Do not use it "just this once." Your savings account is your last resort—the ammo that keeps you from dying, not from simply being "uncomfortable."

It can be terribly difficult to ascribe worth to something you can't see or touch: we buy big-screen TVs because they look pretty on the wall; we buy closets full of clothes because they look good in the fitting room light. Initially, you may not feel the same way about your savings—but you will. It's important to remind yourself of your growing worth:

- Track your balance online.
- Calculate how long your savings would keep you afloat if the worst-case scenario came knocking.
- And, above all else, take pride in the fact that your money is not buying you useless clutter . . . it's buying you freedom: the freedom from debt, the freedom from worry, the freedom from being controlled by anybody else. Your life is your own, but you need money to *keep* it that way.

No one can predict how long a Zombie Economy will last, but with enough preparation, you will outlast it.

A PISTOL IS a fine weapon, to be sure: it's small, relatively lightweight, and can make a handy bludgeon.

It also holds somewhere between six and twenty bullets, depending on the model. Nothing to sneeze at, but not what anyone would call a room-clearer. Its bullets must be fired one at a time, making each round crucial. And no matter how accurate you might be, at the end of your fifteen shots, you've got two choices: run or reload.

For a thicket of ghouls—when they're coming in the windows and down the stairs, filling up the hallways and exits—you need something that will blow an escape route right through the middle. You need force.

You need a machine gun.

A machine gun, in turn, needs bullets—lots of them. Machine guns go through ammunition like movie patrons go through popcorn . . . and like those hideous, shrieking things outside they will go through your soft underbelly, pulling out your stomach while your vision goes dark. Get a pistol. Get a machine gun. And then get all the ammo you can.

WORKSHEET #9: BUILDING YOUR ARSENAL— SETTING AN EMERGENCY SAVINGS GOAL

When it comes to your financial arsenal, typical wisdom says that your savings should equal at least three months' living expenses.

(You should aim for a minimum of six months' worth before you consider channeling any of your money elsewhere, such as any form of investment. More on these subjects can be found at ZombieEconomics.com.)

We'll keep this one simple.

1. FIRST

Go back to the absolute necessities as determined on page 34. Write the monthly average below.

Absolute Necessities Monthly Average: _____

2. NEXT

Below, calculate the *actual amount of savings you must have* to potentially cover one month of living expenses, or two, or three, etc. Simply multiply the absolute necessities figure above by X number of months. Put the result in the third column.

Absolute Necessities Monthly Avg. [From above]	x	Months of Savings	=	Amount You Need to Save
_____	x	1	=	_____
_____	x	2	=	_____
_____	x	3	=	_____
_____	x	4	=	_____
_____	x	5	=	_____
_____	x	6	=	_____
_____	x	7	=	_____
_____	x	8	=	_____

THE END

Select a goal. Write the amount of savings you need to meet that goal in the Key Survival Numbers in the back of the book.

Consider: If you lost your primary income source tomorrow, how long would it take you to find another one? How difficult is the job market? The more problems you anticipate, the more savings you want to have.

THINK OF YOUR EMERGENCY SAVINGS IN TERMS OF THE FIREPOWER IT GIVES YOU

1 month = Hammer

2 months = Hatchet

3 months = Pistol

4 months = Shotgun

5 months = Machine Gun

6 months = All of the above

You place the final box of ammo on the basement shelf and check the bottom of your backpack for strays. Stepping back, you examine your inventory: row upon row of shotgun shells, ammunition for your pistol, a few hatchets, a crowbar, and a double-sided ax. Better safe than sorry, and all that.

You slap your pockets as you walk up the stairs, making sure they hold enough ammo to get you back inside the house, should you be ambushed while outside.

Going from room to room, you check each cabinet and cupboard: ammunition, first-aid kits, and bottles of drinking water are crammed into every available space. Some of the bottles have gone low or empty, and you replenish them from the bathtub, which you keep filled to the brim. Water pressure is only sporadic right now; you expect that it will soon vanish altogether.

Nothing like a few zombies to bring out your inner obsessive-compulsive, your brain says as you stack bottles inside a cupboard.

I have got to get out of this house, you think. *Just for a little while.*

You look toward the front door, wishing desperately that you were anywhere else.

Just for a little while.

CHAPTER FOUR

DON'T GO IN THE GRAVEYARD

HOW AND WHY TO KEEP YOUR JOB . . . EVEN IF YOU HATE IT

Like week-old chewing gum.

Like year-old *Reader's Digest*s.

Like soda left open for a day and a half.

That's what this house feels like.

You know every inch, every corner. You've read every book; you could probably *recite* half of the books. You've counted the number of steps from the bedroom to the bathroom . . . the bathroom to the kitchen . . . the kitchen to the living room, where, for the record, no actual *living* seems to be taking place.

Is this what you're fighting to keep? Is this what your life will be from now on? Will you be seventy years old and still pacing these same rooms, reading the same magazines . . . waiting for something (like death) to relieve the boredom?

You think of the basement, of your ammunition cache. Your house, tiny and cramped though it might feel, is within walking distance of several warehouse-style stores, and one of these features a large selection of hunting supplies. Though the weapons themselves were looted long ago, there are scattered boxes of ammunition strewn throughout the neighborhood. Your best guess is that in the early days of the epidemic, when the infection and insanity seemed to be spreading with equal speed, someone loaded up a truck with guns and bullets. Maybe they thought they could sell or trade these for something else. Maybe they figured with enough guns and ammunition, they didn't *need* to bother with the trading. Whatever the case, they didn't get far—the husk of a burned-out vehicle is just down the road, and for blocks in every direction you can find little boxes of ammunition, along with gun-cleaning supplies and, sometimes, a wristwatch or a ring. As looters ambushed and killed one another, their bounty was spread, little by little, like wreckage on the ocean floor.

And there you are, living near this nexus of plenty. Trapped by good fortune in a miserable, cramped little dwelling, counting ceiling tiles and looking for patterns in the carpet. Wishing you didn't need the ammo so badly. Wishing you could leave.

You stare out the window, debating yourself into the wrong decision.

You need the security. You need the ammo. You need the supplies, your brain reminds you. *You know, the stuff that's here . . . in this house.*

I can find bullets somewhere else, you think. Probably lots of places, considering that the local consumer base has shrunk a bit.

If by "shrunk" you mean "been eaten," then sure, your brain responds. *I'm not really sure that's a ringing endorsement for leaving.*

There's got to be a better house somewhere, you think, *maybe one that's near a gun store or a supermarket.*

Lots of people are hiding in sewers, or just running from place to place, your brain says. *We have a house. Let's keep it.*

I can always come back if things don't work out, you say.

And with that lie, you find yourself gathering supplies. *I can always come back if I don't find something better.*

Your backpack and your pistol loaded, you walk out the front, locking the door behind you. *No sense in taking chances.*

For much of that day, you trudge through one broken, smoldering neighborhood after another. You walk past empty strip malls, their front windows completely gone, past desks and copy machines and office chairs slowly being dissolved by the weather. Past a church with Spanish-styled architecture, the image ruined by several dozen bullet holes and blackened sprays of blood covering the front.

To your left, your peripheral vision catches something glittering. *More glass,* you think. But it's not. It looks like water. A lake.

A lake, your brain scoffs, *now who sounds crazy?*

Undeterred, you walk toward the glitter. As you get closer, you keep squinting: *This can't be real.*

As the pavement gives way to lush, green lawn, you see flower patches . . . trees . . . an oasis. And there, right in the middle, is a small, man-made lake. Everything is overgrown and going wild, but that doesn't matter. Trees mean safety from clawing hands, and a green lawn means water, probably from the same automated system still feeding the lake.

This is amazing.

Then you notice tree stumps—dozens and dozens of them, extending for half a mile in every direction.

Who would be cutting down trees?

You walk toward the lake, your eyes locking onto one of the dark, jutting objects. Your jaw clenches as it comes into focus.

These aren't stumps. They're tombstones. And this is a graveyard.

Your American Dream likely doesn't feature cubicles, time cards, or working endless hours at a job you despise. No one's does. As you shuffle from office to office, as you slog through another all-night shift behind the counter, as you watch the hands on the clock go more and more slowly, you will entertain fantasies of calling it quits. In your mind's eye, you are taking off that apron, throwing down the gas pump, or simply telling your boss that no, you actually *won't* be picking up his morning latte . . . ever again.

Perhaps you decide to *act* on that daydream.

You tell The Man to go to hell, to take his job and shove it, to kiss your grits and forward your mail. You stand tall, shoulders thrown back with pride. You walk past friends and colleagues on your triumphant, principled march out the door.

Then you get home. You call a few more friends. Everyone is at least somewhat supportive. A few of them are ecstatic. You don't notice that these are the same friends who quit *their* jobs . . . and that most of them are still unemployed. You go out for drinks. You sleep late. You wonder about filing for unemployment. You learn you *can't* file for unemployment—that's only for people who've been fired or laid off. You check your savings. You immediately divide it by the cost of your monthly rent. Not as much as you thought.

But then, you're suddenly awash in the golden glow of possibility: the future is yours! Forget working at a job you hate . . . you'll find a better job . . . a *dream* job!

Except that everyone else is *also* looking for those same dream jobs. Some of those people have references, and many of them don't have to omit certain recent employers. A lot of them are still employed, taking their time, crafting just the right letter, just the right approach.

Your friends—the ones who were initially supportive? They can't take much time to celebrate or socialize—they're working. Your *unemployed* friends? They're looking for work—or scared to spend any money. Or both. A few friends will, of course, be happy to drown their sorrows alongside you. You try not to notice how often these conversations leave you feeling depressed and anxious. You think about calling your old employer back; you forcefully disregard what you heard about them filling your position. The calendar seems to slip by. Your savings gets lower—with no unemployment benefits, every month's rent takes a tremendous bite out of what remains.

You wonder if you can get a job *anywhere*. You call friends. They say they'll look into it. They don't call back. You follow up once, and then drop it.

You are in the graveyard . . . and dusk is coming.

The urge to quit an unsatisfying job can be overwhelming, but unless you are moving into a demonstrably better situation, you must resist this urge. Quitting your job can destroy months and years of your life. The satisfaction you feel after telling your boss where to stick it will be short-lived, replaced by an ever-lengthening shadow of worry and doubt.

Right now, someone is muttering "dream killers" under their breath and accusing us of being narrow-minded, joyless, and/or unsympathetic to their hopes and desires. We're not. We're living proof that you can write, talk, plan, or scheme your way into a better place. We're also proof that it takes work. It takes hours and weeks and months of struggle and sacrifice—and those things are far easier to swallow when you're not about to pawn your television.

In the *best* of economic times, it takes, on average, sixteen weeks to find a new job. In a poor economic climate, that time frame expands to thirty-four weeks to a year or more. Those looking for work are sometimes told to anticipate a *yearlong* gap between jobs. That's difficult even when receiving unemployment benefits; without income of any type, it can be disastrous.

When the job market shrinks, the pool of applicants grows. Your job, while undesirable to *you*, may look exceptionally desirable to someone who's been unemployed for six months. In a down economy, your employer may have eliminated that position altogether upon your departure. It may have been farmed out to overseas labor, or divided up among the company's remaining employees. It may still exist, but with a 30 percent reduction in salary. There is no reason to walk into that corpse-filled cemetery unless you must . . . and hating your job just doesn't cut it as a reason.

The Zombie Economy spreads more than distress—it spreads paranoia. It whispers (and sometimes yells), "RUN!" But often, the best decision is to stay put . . . and stay safe.

Below is a worksheet/checklist for those who might be tempted to leave their job. We can't make the decision for you, but these are things you must consider.

Things indicating that you should keep your current job (check those true for you):

_____ Your company has a promising and/or stable future and you are unlikely to be fired.

_____ You have opportunities to advance in this job. (If not now, eventually.)

_____ Health care, a retirement plan, and other significant benefits are included.

_____ You are unlikely to make more money—or gain new skills—by changing to another workplace.

_____ Jobs are scarce in your industry—or for people with your skill set.

_____ You cannot afford to miss a single paycheck.

_____ The unemployment rate (locally and/or nationally) is on the rise . . . or above average.

Things indicating that you can start a job search. (Check those true for you.):

Note: This does not mean it's time to quit. Rather, below are signs that you might be best served by starting a search for another, better job. Do not quit until the next job is firmly in place.

_____ Your company is at risk; layoffs are possible and your job could be eliminated.

_____ There have been specific indications that *you* could be fired.

_____ There is a good market for your skills; there's reason to believe other companies would hire you *now*.

_____ Research says that other companies and/or other positions would pay you significantly more.

_____ Your current salary does not cover your *basic* expenses/ *absolute necessities*.

_____ A different job would likely give you benefits that you don't currently receive.

"YOU ARE NOT your job" goes the saying, and that's true. What's also true is this: How you *perform* your job indicates a great deal about you. Maybe you loathe your boss. Maybe you flat-out detest your customers (maybe you have an inkling that the sentiment goes both ways). All the more reason to drain that job of every nickel you possibly can while working on your dream. All the more reason to *not* get fired. To *not* get demoted. All the more reason—when you finally do secure a better job—to leave on good terms, so as not to jeopardize future offers or opportunities. The world is a closed system, and word travels fast: today's rash outburst is tomorrow's rejection notice.

If all of this sounds demeaning, depressing, or too damned similar to your current situation, then it's time to set some goals. It's time to figure out where you want to be—and what you want to be doing—in a month, and ten months, and a hundred months.

We can't answer that question for you, but we can say this: What could possibly be more satisfying than using someone *else's* money to get what you want?

Remember: Companies—of any size—are interested in one thing above all others . . . making money. If you show ambition, creativity, and/or dedication, you take a small step toward making yourself indispensable, and that can eventually mean enough ammunition (money) to leave the stifling little house once and for all. Even if you don't plan to *be* with the company in the long run, you need to leave on your own terms. When cutbacks are made, having impressed your bosses could make the difference between employment and unemployment.

YOU MAY RESTOCK shelves all day, but that income makes it easier to be a musician when you're away from work. You may process insurance claims from nine to five, but that money allows you to run a website devoted to comic books and collectibles—a website you're hoping to grow into a moneymaker. You must put your life in perspective, separating your passions from the work that is sometimes necessary to fuel them.

Find books—especially biographies or autobiographies—of those who made an impact in your dream field. You'll find an astonishing number of stories similar to your own: striving, suffering, and plowing through every stifling, uninspiring day at a soul-crushing job. They escaped, sometimes through luck, sometimes through backbreaking work, and, more often than not, through a combination of the two.

Entertainment can be found anywhere. Here are some zero-cost suggestions for making it through the daily grind:

- Using specific unpleasant job duties as the currency, place bets with your coworkers regarding customer behavior or clothing. If job duties aren't swappable, bet using push-ups instead of cash. The loser must, at the winner's request, perform X number of push-ups at the first available moment. This continues until all of the push-ups have been worked off.
- Post something provocative/inflammatory/compelling on an Internet message board before work, and then envision the responses that will be waiting when you return home.

- Stuck behind the counter at a coffee shop? Use it as your chance to examine the broad spectrum of humanity. Write a blog describing what one can learn about society from observing coffee shop behavior. Better yet, take notes, refine them, and write a book proposal.
- If you're chained to a desk all day, find out if your company allows earphones (or listening to something other than the piped-in elevator music). Sample one new radio show or podcast every single day; within a matter of weeks, you'll have a bounty of entertainment to accompany your daily drudge.

When all is said and done, your job is just that—a job. It's something you must be able to turn off from time to time, or it will infiltrate every moment of your life, eventually snuffing out the enjoyable moments you *do* have.

If you find yourself obsessing about your job during your downtime/off-hours—especially if it's a job you dislike—it's time to take control of your thoughts. Your mind is like any other muscle: it can be made stronger, and it can learn to shut out your workplace when you're not working. This won't happen overnight; your mind takes time to master any new skill. What's key is not to scold yourself or give in to frustration when you find yourself dwelling on work, or work-related stress. When you discover that your day job has crept into your off-time thoughts, simply move your thoughts back to where they were before, or to something completely new. This isn't mystical gibberish or pseudo-spiritual nonsense: your neurons are trainable, and this mental refocusing will eventually become automatic. Keep at it, slowly and steadily, and your brain will free itself from workplace shackles.

Just as important, make sure to really *use* your time away from work. This doesn't always mean starting a massive project or detailing the next ten years of your life (though it certainly can). What it does mean is letting your brain unwind, and letting your true self out to breathe. After all, escaping that terrible job only benefits you if there's some actual "you" left . . . so don't allow your job to smother your life.

Do the things you always *claim* you're going to do:

Pick up that graphic novel you've heard about, marathon your favorite movies, have a board-game night with your friends, actually *start* your novel, actually *write* that amazing song, actually *begin* that screenplay.

WORKSHEET #11: FINDING FULFILLMENT OUTSIDE OF WORK

Fighting the Zombie Economy can require all of your strength; it will burn your muscles and scrape your skin. It will make you want to quit. And that is when you are most at risk.

In order to survive, you must want to survive, and that's far easier when your life has some measure of fulfillment. If this already describes you, congratulations—skip this worksheet and plunge ahead. But if you wish for a little more motivation, this worksheet is for you. Everyone has a reason to live. Let's find yours.

1. FIRST

List three things you wish you were doing instead of filling out this worksheet:

_____

_____

_____

2. NEXT

When you read, watch television, or go online, what kinds of things most draw your attention? Give three examples:

_____

_____

_____

3. NEXT

List three things—big or small, everyday or extraordinary—that you want to try or accomplish. These can be specific ("learn the rarified art of chain saw carving") or vague ("focus on something more artistic than my day job").

_____

_____

_____

THE END

Now it's time to act. Pick one of the above interests or goals and take a step toward making it happen. For many (if not most) of these items, you'll find that reading about it comes first—and reading can, of course, be a fine end in and of itself.

Join a group. Start a group. Look for a series of free lessons or classes. Whatever your interest, there's a way to start working toward it *now*. Even if cost delays the actual completion, the thought process and preparation will have given you invaluable energy and motivation. Your thoughts and state of mind will be aided immeasurably, making it easier to survive the time between "now" and "then."

NO ONE EXPECTS you to stay in a miserable job forever. At least, *we* don't.

We also don't expect you to walk away from a steady supply of ammunition. If you do, you will regret it.

You will regret it the first time you get an eviction or repossession notice. You will regret it the first time you have to ask your parents for money. You will regret it the first time you realize you've been living on credit cards . . . and they start coming up "declined."

Gather your ammo, store your ammo, study the landscape, and wait. Your moment of action will come . . . if you survive long enough to see it.

Don't go in the graveyard.

As you stare at the tombstones, the vision of your oasis vanishes into the hot, still air. You're filled with a bleak terror—you expect an attack to come at any moment. You compulsively recheck your grip on the pistol.

Let's get back home, your brain says.

You couldn't agree more.

With society in chaos, there has been no reliable source for information; it's impossible to sort fact from fiction. From speculation. From insanity. Occasionally, you have crossed paths with other survivors, each one of them with a different version of the truth. It's painfully clear that no one knows anything, least of all what's causing this . . . *nightmare.*

You *do* know that the last place you're going to put yourself is in a graveyard, walking a few feet above thousands of possible zombies.

No thank you—the house is fine, you think. It's not ideal; it's not where you want to be in fifteen years, but it's where you need to be right now.

You weigh your options: go home by the same route that got you here, or take a different road.

Taking the familiar path has obvious advantages: you're less likely to get lost, and unless something has changed in the past half hour, it should still be free of zombies.

On the other hand, you've searched most of the buildings on that route; it's doubtful you'd find any new food or weapon stashes.

Your stomach growls.

Your brain chimes in: *I could go for some cheese fries.*

I'll keep an eye out, you reply, adjusting your backpack. You head down the left-hand road, into uncharted territory.

The city's streets have a strange, alien feel to them, like your high school when you visit ten years after graduating. Vaguely familiar storefronts, signs that seem to be on the wrong corner—you're soon walking much slower than you'd planned, making sure you don't miss anything.

Cars fill the road. Some of them empty. Some of them empty and burned to a crisp. Some of them containing zombies, like a horrible, giant box of Cracker Jack. *Thank God for seat belts,* you think, as you pass by these cars, their undead occupants lunging at you through shattered windows. You put a bullet in their brains before the moaning attracts their pals.

Vehicles of every size are smashed into buildings, into telephone poles, into one another. They straddle concrete barriers and sidewalks, the blockage ten cars wide in some places, snaking ahead in one solid glut as far as you can see.

What typically happened was this: a family member was sick, infected . . . but not yet fully transformed. The rest of the family would try to get them to a hospital, or out of the city altogether, maybe thinking they could find a cure somewhere. The infected person lapsed into a coma, then went berserk, attacking everyone else in the car. The car would crash, usually in the middle of the road. That caused a pileup, then a traffic jam. Meanwhile, more people who didn't know about the traffic jam turned down the same road, immediately getting stuck. At some point, a zombie would escape from a car and bite the first person it saw. With all the chaos and nowhere to run, a swarm of zombies was soon attacking everything. People still inside their cars would roll up the windows, and they'd either die that way or they'd go delirious from hunger and dehydration . . . rolling the windows back down to order something from the dead, staggering waitress.

Threading your way down the sidewalk, you scan both sides of the street, looking at storefronts. Unbroken glass typically means a shop hasn't been looted already; there's a much better chance of finding something valuable inside.

There aren't many unbroken windows these days.

Something emerges about a hundred yards away, on the other side of the street. It's a storefront . . . covered in big sheets of plywood, even the front doors.

That was done from the outside, you think.

Which means . . . your brain begins.

No one's inside. Some store owners covered their storefronts with big panels of wood before fleeing, thinking they'd return before any serious looting could begin.

Wrong.

A cover job like this also meant the store was empty. No people inside, and no zombies, either, since the owner would have just *shot* them, rather than trapping them.

The sheets of wood look intact—no one's been inside.

You do a 360 check and then cross the street, staying clear of car windows and watching the ground for partial zombies . . . a lesson learned while reinforcing your house. Horrible, damaged creatures with no legs still have plenty of teeth.

Visible above the nail-filled plywood, the sign reads:

THOMPSON'S 24-HOUR MARKET

CANDIES—CIGARETTES—SODA—BEER—SUNDRIES

What the hell is a sundry? asks your brain.

You don't know and you don't take the time to answer. You're inserting your hatchet blade between two pieces of paneling, prying the store wide open.

CHAPTER FIVE

THEY'LL EAT THE FAT ONES FIRST

FITNESS AS A FINANCIAL ASSET

Oh, my God, your brain says, as you pry back the thin wooden sheeting that covers the convenience store.

You're hard-pressed to disagree. Even with just a couple inches' worth of sunlight streaming into the store, you can see heaven.

Rows and rows of cellophane-wrapped snacks, candy, desserts, single-serving lunches . . . and that's just what's visible. Your heart races at the sight of so much food . . . all untouched, all still sealed and fresh.

Your brain stifles a giggle. *Right . . . fresh. Like cream filling is a food group. You know that stuff never expires. They've done lab tests.*

That's an urban legend, you respond, curling your hands around the bottom corner of a panel and pulling. *The expiration date—*

With a loud squeal, a sheet of plywood above your head tears loose. You press against the storefront, waiting for the huge panel to fall into the street. Instead, it comes straight down like a falling elevator . . . the nails that jut from the back catching your forearm, tearing out long strips of skin. The wood panel cracks into the ground and comes to rest in a cloud of dust, pinning you against the storefront.

You scream, not even thinking to hold it in. You sink to your knees, clutching your arm, dimly aware of other nails digging into your arms as you collapse. With your body no longer supporting it, the panel slips, falling into the glass doors, which shatter with a deafening crash; you're covered in a rain of sharp glass fragments.

Dammit, dammit, dammit . . .

Your arm is streaming blood. And, even worse . . .

Could we have made more noise? your brain asks.

Goddammit. You look inside the store. You see the aisles of un-touched, perfect little packages.

You look down at your arm, tiger stripes of bright red, dripping onto the ground. You look at the wood panel, leaning back, halfway through the glass door, nails spiking through the back.

You look closer: at least some of the nails appear to be caked in rust. Or is it blood?

We have to go, your brain says, *something wicked will be coming this way.*

Sure enough, you hear a moan from somewhere down the road. Then two.

With an old-man grunt, you stand. You check your pistol and backpack and head back the way you came.

You try not to think about the blood coming out of your arm. You *really* try not to think about the rust that might be coursing through your system. *What does that even do?* You can't quite remember. *Makes you sick, or gives you . . .*

Lockjaw.

You groan a little, despite yourself. *Perfect. That's fantastic. Great.*

You wonder when the last time you had a tetanus shot was.

You wonder about all the blood dripping from your arm. You pause, check your surroundings, and take a closer look at the wound: the bleeding doesn't seem to be stopping or even slowing.

The nails destroyed your shirt's left sleeve; you pull a lightweight jacket from your backpack and wrap it around the damaged fore-arm; you don't want to leave a trail of bread crumbs for whatever's behind you.

Your stomach churns again. You consider pulling some food out of your pack, but with your left arm injured and your right hand holding the gun, that wouldn't give you many hands left, and you need to get moving.

You think about the food in the store. Bags and bags and cans and cans. Your whole life seems to come out of a tin at this point. After the power started failing, all the fresh food rotted . . . supermarket display cases filled with big, gray slabs of fuzz-covered mystery. No farms, no gardens that you know of . . . and you're guessing they'd be grown over by now anyway. No one's left to tend them. Nature is slowly taking things back. Nature and the undead, divvying up the city like gangland shot-callers: *You take downtown, I'll take the west side.*

Your arm throbs. You wonder about gangrene. And whether the living dead are filling the air with some kind of germ or spore. Some kind of . . . *zombie dust* that just floats around, into your lungs, into open wounds—

You force yourself to focus. *Just . . . keep walking.*

It is an open wound, though, says your brain, sounding like the Good Cop. *It's going to be trouble one way or another if we don't take care of it.*

You think about your puny first-aid kit. A few bandages, a pair of scissors, motion-sickness pills.

You shake your head. You stop. You look around.

You sling off your backpack and reach inside, pulling out a map. Squinting at the nearby street signs, you look down at the legend in the map's corner . . . then to the grid of street names.

About a mile and a half away is a community hospital. Probably not that big, but that might be okay; the bigger hospitals were over-run pretty early. That's when things really started to go haywire. Too many people, and not enough anything.

Far off in the distance, somewhere, you hear what sounds like an engine.

You listen. Minutes pass. Nothing.

You look at your left arm. Blood is already spotting through the jacket.

You stand for a moment longer, then you head for the hospital.

Standing in the parking lot of Gracen Hospital, you see an almost comical portrait of desertion: vans with their doors hanging open, a row of empty, identical cars that say "Coroner's Office" on the side, paper blowing everywhere, and, hanging above the main entrance, a bedsheet sign:

WE CAN'T HELP YOU

You stare at the sign, and then at the entrance . . . unsure.

The ground floor of the hospital is lined with windows; you walk closer to peer inside. No sense entering a roach motel.

Especially if it's filled with spiders, your brain adds.

Your right hand ready with the pistol, you step onto the sidewalk and put your face to the glass, cupping your left hand around your eyes.

The hospital is filled with garbage: paper cups and plates, lots of clothes, piles of what might be dirt.

You strain your eyes, looking for movement. Nothing.

Maybe it's an out-of-network provider, says your brain.

Squinting through the glass, you see a wide hallway straight ahead, just past the admissions desk.

You step back from the window and look up: it's a three-story building.

Something catches your eye. From inside a third-floor office a lone zombie stares down at you—its palms banging against the glass as its mouth bites at the smooth, clear surface.

You're chewing the inside of your lower lip, looking from the third-floor zombie to the ground level . . . which seems empty.

You peel a layer of wrapping from your arm. Blood drips onto the asphalt.

Shouldn't it be clotting or something by now?

You wonder if your body even has the ability to heal itself at this point. Your diet hasn't been all that balanced.

The ghoul bangs at the window.

Your body keeps bleeding.

You walk toward the entrance.

Can we be blunt?

If you smoke, you're doing the zombies' job for them.

If you abuse yourself with drugs or alcohol, or stuff yourself full of fattening foods, with no regard for your poor body's increasingly futile attempts to keep itself alive . . . you will die. It might be fast, or it might take a long, long time.*

Your body is an amazing machine—the most elaborate, complex mechanism on Earth. It needs to be—everything that walks, swims, crawls, flies, or lurches is fighting for the apex position on the food chain.

Your body needs every trick it's got, because nothing else out there will cut it an inch of slack.

In issues of fitness, as in issues of economy, one immutable fact remains:

No one is coming to save you.

Your finances and your health are intertwined, to put it mildly. Your health allows you to work and, hopefully, to prosper. The rewards of that prosperity allow you to take better care of yourself and your loved ones as the inevitable ravages of aging, environment, and bad luck take their toll.

Lose or damage your health, and your financial stability can soon follow. It's easy to find yourself in a spiraling nightmare of medical bills, diminished income, and physical deterioration—each of them exacerbating the others.

Let's be clear: the world is a dangerous place. Any number of people are stricken—sometimes at birth—with debilitating, excruciating

---

* As a special bonus to your loved ones, your slow death means they'll get to worry, and cry, and take care of your mangled, overworked, mistreated body while it gradually falls apart. If you've really managed to make a spectacular wreck of things, the person who shares your bed might get to tend to your bathroom needs.

diseases. Every day, scores of those who made the *right* choices are victims of chance, heredity, or the passing of years.

There are lots of things out there waiting for the chance to hurt you—whether you deserve it or not. Putting yourself in danger by *willfully* mistreating your body is selfish, disrespectful, and unacceptably stupid.

It's also bad business.

WHY YOUR HEALTH IS A FINANCIAL ISSUE

Preventable chronic diseases are costly. Let us count the ways:

AT THE HOSPITAL
- Medication
- Stopgap or "temp" cures (such as heart stents, which must be replaced over time)
- Maintenance treatments (such as dialysis)

ON THE JOB
- Income lost due to illness
- Sick days also scream "weakness" and/or "liability" to many employers.

IN YOUR PERSONAL ECONOMY
- Someone who is chronically ill doesn't have the same energy to manage their finances or career because they are weakened by the sickness itself. Additionally, time spent managing the disease is time *not* spent managing their job/money.

- Medical bills are the single largest reason for personal bankruptcies. The single largest reason for *medical bills*? Preventable **Chronic Disease.**[†]

STILL NOT CONVINCED?

- We're going to take a wild guess here: You probably *don't* want to end up in a nursing home. Most hospital stays and most nursing home admissions are related to *preventable* chronic diseases.

Remember that fact.

Write it on your refrigerator or in the drawer where you keep your cigarettes: "I don't want to spend the last ten years of my life in a *nursing home*."

When Congress passed health reform in 2010, it allowed employers to lower your premiums 30 to 50 percent *if* you enter a wellness program and meet certain goals for health factors such as weight and cholesterol level.

Check to see if your company is doing this now or is even *considering* this. It could be a rare double-zombie kill: saving money *and* making you stronger.

It works both ways, of course: *not* meeting these goals could cost workers/families thousands of dollars a year.

[†] **Chronic Disease** (*noun*): A disease that is recurring or long-lasting (defined as a minimum of three months, though these are often lifelong ailments). Nearly one in ten Americans has a chronic disease.

TRAVELING THROUGH THE zombie apocalypse, one encounters ghouls in numerous forms, each of them dangerous in its own way, each requiring a specific kind of defense:

Zombies trapped inside a building, howling and moaning at survivors who pass nearby. The key: keep moving. Don't enter the building, and don't linger nearby.

Damaged or severely decomposed zombies, unable even to crawl, remaining shrouded by an overgrown field or in a pile of rubble. The key: such areas must be searched carefully and, when possible, avoided altogether.

Zombies who have lost their windpipes and voice boxes to injury or decay. Lacking the physical capability to produce a zombie's telltale moan, these specimens give little audible warning of their approach, emitting only a ragged, wet gasp. Beyond an inadvertent stealth, this condition carries another danger: because such creatures are unable to vocalize—and thus, unable to attract other zombies to their location—they are often alone, rather than traveling in an easily spotted swarm. The key: pure and simple vigilance. Check your surroundings constantly. Make as little noise as possible. Always give yourself an escape route.

In a similar fashion, the three most common chronic diseases can, to a large extent, be avoided by changes in your behavior. These are things *you can control*, things you have the power to alter, and doing so will save your health—and a ton of money.

Protect yourself. If you give these monsters the upper hand, they'll take your whole body.

TYPE 2 DIABETES

Arguably the most common of all preventable chronic diseases.

What it will do to you—It decreases wound healing. It can destroy feeling in your extremities. If it goes unchecked, it can lead to multiple amputations. It *will* lead to multiple hospitalizations. Oh . . . and it can also cause you incredible, permanent pain as it destroys your nerves.

What it will cost you—Diabetics have to check their blood sugar levels regularly to monitor fluctuations, or risk lapsing into a diabetic coma. Testing involves pricking your finger with a small blade, putting the blood on a testing strip, then inserting the testing strip into a small machine. The machine is a onetime expense, but the testing strips and blades have an *ongoing* price tag that some insurance won't cover . . . and diabetics need as many as four strips and blades a day. Additionally, diabetics must pay for medications such as insulin,[*] oral blood sugar regulators, and high-glucose tabs (to raise blood sugar should it fall below normal).

People with diagnosed diabetes incur average medical costs nearly *150 percent higher* than those without diabetes. Remember: This cost won't show up immediately . . . and neither will the savings. Both accrue over time, like bad (or good) credit scores.

Why you? You're at great risk for diabetes if:

- You have relatives with diabetes.
- You're over forty-five.
- And most important, if you're overweight.

While the first two factors are unalterable, the third is preventable and crucial. Obesity is a large enough factor that if you get your weight under control *even after being diagnosed with diabetes*, it's possible to reverse it altogether, and go off all medications.

Prevention—Don't get fat. This means avoiding processed sugars and processed carbs. Eat large amounts of vegetables, fruits, lean proteins, and legumes (such as lentils, beans, and peas). When you eat

---

[*] And the razor-sharp needles with which it's injected.

grains (e.g., bread, pasta, cereal), eat *whole* grains—those that haven't been bleached, fried, or doused with suspicious chemicals.*

Also: exercise. But you knew that. (For tips on foods that maximize the effect of your workout, go to ZombieEconomics.com.)

> You can reduce your risk of developing Type 2 diabetes by 58 percent by eating healthfully and exercising at moderate intensity for thirty minutes each day. Likewise, calorie restriction can reduce body weight by 5 to 7 percent, yielding a 60 percent reduction in risk.

HEART DISEASE

Heart disease is the alpha zombie of illnesses. It's incredibly costly . . . if it doesn't kill you first. The Centers for Disease Control list heart disease as the number-one cause of death in the United States. (Contrary to widespread belief, heart disease is the number-one killer of women, surpassing breast cancer.)

What it will do to you—Heart disease can mean a horde of ailments, including: high blood pressure, high cholesterol, chronic heart failure, and coronary artery disease . . . all of which can lead to a heart attack and/or a stroke (leaving you, in turn, with severe speech, memory, and/or mobility problems).

What it will cost you—If you let heart disease into your life, the costs are enormous and grow as the disease progresses. Cholesterol medication, blood pressure pills, doctors' visits, blood tests, echocar-

---

* This is true regardless of whatever insane diet craze is sweeping the populace. More on this later in the chapter.

diograms, electrocardiograms, stress tests, MRIs and other image scans. Strokes are the single biggest cause of long-term disability, forcing some victims to depend on others for their care.

Why you? You're at great risk for heart disease if:

- You eat a diet heavy in fats and/or processed foods.
- You are obese.
- You smoke.
- You suffer from high blood pressure (which is, in turn, caused by and/or aggravated by the above three).

Prevention—Similar to diabetes prevention: diet and exercise. Don't overwhelm your heart with a poor diet or a huge body to lug around, and voilà—your heart endures less strain.

LUNG DISEASE

For those of you who prefer to spend your last years (and perhaps decades) rasping for breath, carting around an oxygen tank, growing fistfuls of revolting tumors inside your lungs, and, for a finale, feeling like you're drowning—*all the time*—nothing beats cigarettes.* If you feel like these are things you'd rather avoid, don't smoke, and minimize the time you spend around those who are smoking.

 EAT TO LIVE . . . OR LIVE TO BE EATEN

We're not going to spend a lot of time on this point for one simple reason: you already know.

Eat sensibly and in moderation.

---

* Men may also receive the extra prize of becoming impotent.

> Allow yourself to indulge from time to time.
>
> Exercise.
>
> Repeat.
>
> If you ignore this, or stray from it for long periods of time, you will gain weight. Maybe a lot of it. The more weight you gain, the greater your chance of dying and/or going broke keeping yourself alive.

DIET IS CRUCIAL. *Diets* are crap.

Let's be crystal clear on this point:

GOOD FOR YOU

- Fruits and vegetables
- Whole grains (not white bread painted brown; things such as oats or whole wheat)
- Legumes
- Low- or no-fat dairy (with cheese, this means tending toward white varieties, such as mozzarella)

And, for you carnivores, some lean meats:

- Ground turkey
- Lean pork chops or pork tenderloin
- Chicken, especially in thin cutlets
- Beef; leaner cuts include strip steak, T-bone steak, and tenderloin; the leanest cuts include top sirloin and top round.

WILL MAKE YOU FAT AND WEAK

- Processed sugars (read: 99 percent of candies/sodas)
- Large amounts of fatty meats (primarily red meat)
- Trans fats (found in most sweet or salty vending-machine type snacks)

- Alcohol
- Large amounts of salt/sodium
- Large servings of dairy

Any diet that contradicts the above is definitely deceptive, possibly dangerous, and will *not* lead to long-term weight loss. There is, however, an industry built on reinterpreting this information in confusing and terrifying ways.

AREAS OF PARTICULAR DANGER

- **Any diet that focuses on eating only—or mostly—one specific food.** The cabbage soup diet will only last as long as your willpower . . . and your willpower sucks, or you wouldn't be fishing around for a quick-fix weight solution.
- **Any diet based on one kind of food.** Similar to the above, but centered on a particular "category," such as protein. These are often targeted at men, because they offer the chance to overindulge. (You know the sort of thing we're talking about: the all-sausage-and-big-slabs-of-cheese diet.) This approach *will* work well as long as you are on it, but unless you can tolerate meat and eggs for life (and you can't . . . just ask your heart), you will soon have to learn how to deal with a piece of toast or an apple, and that tends to go poorly if your tongue has been in a sensory-deprivation tank for six months.

  We are meant to consume a wide variety of real foods, and if any diet preaches against this, you are being lied to.
- **Any diet that *sells* you the food involved,** or recommends

> a certain *brand* of food. Run for the door. And check
> your wallet on the way out.
>
> • **Any diet based overwhelmingly on shakes, bars,
> powders, pills.** These are often the most expensive
> diets on Earth because you rely on one business to
> provide your basic nutritional needs. They will charge
> you infinitely more for their trademarked, powdered
> concoction than the real foods it is meant to replicate.

If you feel you need more information regarding diet and nutrition, or if you have specific dietary needs (such as a vegan regimen), read *health* books . . . *not* diet books. When in doubt, ask a librarian, and be specific: say you want a book (preferably a textbook) on nutrition.

> Remember: All weight loss comes down to calorie
> reduction—burning more calories than you consume.
> There are no exceptions to this. At all.

> Do not:
> • Buy any large piece of exercise equipment. There are
> too many treadmills-turned-clothing-hangers in the
> world to justify even one more purchase.

- Buy any exercise equipment until you establish a routine . . . and have stuck to that routine for at least two months.
- Immediately join a gym or health spa. Investigate pay-per-play options. Give yourself a trial period to see if you will actually get your money's worth. If you are sure you will use a gym, it is a great investment. But only if you use it. If a gym doesn't offer or won't consider a pay-as-you-go membership, that tells you something: not even *they* seriously expect that you'll stick with the plan; that's why they want their money up front.)

Regarding Health Insurance

If you do not have insurance, your life—both literally and figuratively—is on a rickety platform. You know this. So do we.

Do not throw things further off balance by living dangerously.

We're not your mom, your dad, your guidance counselor, or your priest. We're not here to pass moral judgment or make your life less interesting. We're here to make sure you live long enough to have a shot at prosperity.

If you behave recklessly, it will cost you. You do *not* have the nine lives afforded to folks with health care. You get one strike, if you're lucky. Screw up more than that, and you'll spend the rest of your life in a paper hat, serving orange soda to teenagers and living paycheck to paycheck.

You cannot take chances with your health if you are uninsured.

Bitter? Angry? Jealous of those who can afford (or were given) health care? You won't prove anything by dying young or dying broke.

Treat yourself like a survivor, because no one else will.

If you have insurance, congratulations. Use it. Don't delay or postpone, because that coverage—especially if it's a function of your job—could vanish overnight.

Get your teeth cleaned, filled, or whatever else they need.

Get a physical and any annual/regular checkups. If you have a family history of some particular ailment, make sure to ask the doctor about age of onset and possible symptoms . . . and when you need to start watching out for them.

And, though it should go without saying . . . keep your job.

If you do not have insurance, it is even more important that you:

- **Take your vitamins.** This doesn't require joining a club or going to some freak-filled vitamin store. Just buy a massive bottle of multivitamins—generics are fine—and take one every day. If you're vegan/vegetarian, add some additional B vitamins to the mix.
- **Sleep.** There is no magic number, but you probably need more than you're getting. Too little will make you sick and dull your decision-making capability.
- **Take care of your teeth.** Brush at least twice a day. Yes, flossing sucks. Do it anyway. Tip: do it while watching TV at night. Don't wait until you're asleep on the couch and drooling, or it won't get done.
- **Do your own self-screenings.** Many hospitals and clinics offer free lessons/information about self-checks for

breast cancer, testicular cancer, skin cancers, etc. Women should talk to a local nonprofit clinic or women's health organization for information on free or reduced-cost yearly checkups. (For more information, go to Zombie Economics.com.)

- **Drink water.** Guess what? If you feel dehydrated, you've already been that way for some time. Drink small amounts throughout the day. Do not buy bottled water. Get a permanent bottle, fill it, and keep it with you.
- **Limit fast food.** Limit to as close to none as possible.
- **Control your vices.** If you are a recreational drug user or drinker, keep a close eye on your intake; don't let it get the upper hand.
- **If you are struggling with addiction, or have a tendency to binge, it's time to get a handle on things.** Seek help, or it will cost you a great deal of money, productivity, and health.
- **Wear protection.** Use your seat belt. Your motorcycle helmet. Your bike helmet. Your condom (see next point). Your sunscreen. All these things were created to save you from health risks and hardships. Not using *any* of them just *once* could be a life-altering, financially devastating event.
- **Have safe sex, or don't have sex at all.** There are no other options. And the truth is: The only guaranteed way of avoiding sexually transmitted disease and unwanted pregnancy is to not have sex.
- **If you are struggling financially and don't have children . . . *don't have children*.** Again, either use birth control or don't have sex. Having kids while in dire fiscal

straits is stress-inducing for the parent(s), damaging to the child, and risks permanent doom for everyone involved.

IS IT CRUCIAL TO GET HEALTH INSURANCE?

If you *can* get health insurance, you absolutely should. But if you are so tight on cash that this would come at the expense of other necessities, consider these questions to help you prioritize:

1. How old are you? (Younger people are less prone to illness; their use of insurance is often for major, unexpected health concerns.)
2. Do children or others depend on you?
3. What would you have to give up to afford health insurance? Consider different levels of insurance, from full coverage to basic-catastrophic coverage.

If at all possible, try to have at least catastrophic coverage.

Physical concerns—like financial concerns—are an unavoidable fact of life, and are something for which you *must* prepare.

The zombies are coming for your money. Misfortune and time are coming for your health. Surrender either of these things . . . and you will lose them both.

The door is the manual kind—*thank you, God*—and it pulls open with no noise.

You step inside. The admissions desk, like everything else, is covered with office trash, though the "ring for service" bell is still in place. You wonder who rang it last, and what they wanted.

Flexing your fingers, you step through the clutter and past the desk, heading down the hallway; it ends in a T about thirty feet down. The left turn is blocked; right takes you down another corridor.

The corridor's left side is lined with small exam rooms. All the doors are shut. On the right, about twenty paces ahead, a large, open set of double doors leads into a room with several gurneys. Next to each one, you see curtains pulled back in a bunch.

An emergency room, you think, *or something close enough.*

Your pain-filled arm seems to throb with its own pulse. You walk through the wide doorway, relaxing when you see no other entrances.

Or exits, your brain reminds you.

Good point. You move quickly, opening drawers and cabinets. The third drawer comes up lucky—you find a collection of what look like oversized pieces of classroom chalk, pointed at one end. Styptic pencils. Used by men the world over on shaving nicks. Press the tip to the injury, and the bleeding stops, instantly.

And they hurt like hell. But they work.

You don't stop to think. You tear the plastic off one of the pointed white cylinders, and then unwrap your arm. You look at the wound.

This is really going to hu—

Using the styptic pencil like a rolling pin, you press it down against one of the bloody patches, moving it back and forth over the wound, again and again. It's like holding your arm above a flame. You do it twice more, once for each jagged rip in your forearm. When you're done, tears are squeezing from your eyes. You press a towel to your arm, now a chalky white over deep, blackened red. The towel comes up spotted, but mostly dry; the bleeding is nearly stopped.

You exhale.

No time.

You open every drawer. Bandages, medical tape, some things that might be splints, masks, gloves, rubbing alcohol, more styptic pencils.

You think of the nails, the rust. You have no idea where antibiotics are even *kept*. Or painkillers, and you have a dim suspicion you'll be needing some of those, too.

You circle the room once more, cinch your pack closed, and put it over your shoulders. You pick up the pistol, walk out the double doors, and turn right, continuing down the hallway. All paths seem to lead to the lobby, and who knows . . . you might pass the pharmacy on the way.

Your boot kicks something small, and there's a ringing, chiming echo: a bullet casing, bouncing down the tile hallway. *Dammit*.

You look down at the ground; more than a few of them.

All right, walk carefully.

A shrill, whining noise—too thin and high to be a ghoul—wafts from somewhere.

You stop.

Cats.

You think of the notices that used to be stenciled on condemned tenement houses: "If animal trapped, call . . ." and then a phone number.

You hear the sound again.

Well, why not cats? you think. *Nature isn't just trees and zombies; let 'em all fight for their turn.*

You wonder what the world will look like in fifteen years . . . in twenty.

You keep walking, careful not to bump or kick anything else. Cats make noise, and noise brings other things. *And that's something we can do without.*

Then you see the shoes. Connected to legs. Stretched out on the floor.

You freeze in mid-step. Your breathing stops, and your finger tightens on the trigger.

A second ticks by . . . then two, then three. The creature doesn't move.

You look more closely: black shoes leading to gray pants leading to a shirt, all of it wrapped around a man in his mid-forties. Dead.

Eyes open, but with a crater-sized gunshot wound through the side of his head. No bites, no scratches, no sign of infection.

Suicide, you think, and keep walking. You see another pair of shoes straight ahead. They're attached to a woman—dead from a similar head wound.

Next to her, a man in his late twenties, shot cleanly through the forehead, with no sign of infection. His right hand hold hers; his left hand holds a photo album.

By the time you've gone another ten yards, the bodies cover the floor, sometimes two or three slumped into a pile. All dead. None from zombie attacks. *Some kind of mass suicide,* you think, *but why* here?

Does anything really need a reason at this point? asks your brain, rhetorically.

Fair enough, you think in response. You look around. You've had enough of this place. Time to go.

The shrill whine has returned, louder than before.

You don't wait. You move past the bodies, stepping over and around them. You'll find some other pharmacy, some other time.

The hallway ends in a right turn. You're past the skylights now; you have to strain to make out your surroundings. Peering down the corridor, you see a faint light ahead, maybe a hundred feet. The lobby. The outside.

You hear movement behind you, where you just came from. You suddenly wonder why you're here, *why did this seem like such a goddamned important idea—?*

Because you were bleeding to death, your brain replies.

Never again, you vow, starting down the dark hallway, headed toward the dim glow.

Something clatters behind you. You step faster. There are bodies everywhere; your boots are clumsy in the half-dark, coming down on hands and hanks of hair.

More clattering, like someone banging a metal tray.

Your foot catches on something and you trip, stumbling forward. Your knees hit the hard, flat tile. Your hands splay out to break your fall and land in what feels like baker's dough, warm from the oven.

Above the shrill, fractured whining of the cats, something is shrieking. The echoing makes it impossible to figure out where the sound is coming from.

Clenching your jaw until your teeth creak, you crawl forward. *Don't think, don't think, don't think,* you tell yourself, your hands and knees traveling across mounds of yielding decay.

The light gets brighter as you near the hallway's end. You keep crawling, not wanting to risk another fall in semidarkness.

The corridor banks left, and you are suddenly bathed in light. Still on your knees, you look up. You're directly underneath an interior window. On the other side of the glass, a small room: pale-green walls, the shadowy flicker of dying fluorescent bulbs.

Emergency lighting, not sunlight.

You've been crawling deeper into the core of the hospital.

The mewling, wailing, cat sound . . . the strangled yowl of civilized things gone wild . . . is coming from everywhere. You rise up just enough to peer through the window and into the room. You see boxes of latex gloves, rubber tubing, pieces of hospital equipment—most of it damaged. Something that looks like a wall clock has been torn from the plaster; it dangles from a few thin wires.

You don't see anyone inside. Your sight line goes all the way to the back wall—it's empty.

The yowling increases, like a dozen band saws squealing their way through thick, knotted wood.

This is not an exit.

You have to turn around . . . you have to go back, and whatever is making that clattering noise . . . you'll shoot it, you'll step over its decomposing body, and you'll get the hell out.

Then let's stop crawling, your brain suggests.

One, two, three—

You stand up. You look through the window into the flickering room.

Your thoughts go completely offline for several moments, like a computer rebooting after a power surge. Then the room and its contents fade back into view.

You see them laid out in rows and rows, like little, see-through coffins—each one holding a small, writhing occupant with dry, chalk-white eyes and gaping, ragged injuries. Some are barely more than a mound of entrails and a moaning, screaming mouth.

You see shattered, overturned piles of Plexiglas and blankets. A miniature hand vanishes into a tangle of plastic and pink cloth.

Something comes from the back of the room, straight toward you, and slams against the glass. You see a name tag, you see wet, rancid streaks against the window. You see a gun in the background. You wonder who it was for.

Your vision goes soft around the edges. A buzzing noise fills your ears and your mind, blocking the shrieks and tiny, splintered screaming. Your surroundings are muffled and distant as you turn from the window . . . from the snapping, biting, name-tag-wearing thing.

You walk back through the hallways, retracing your path . . . not stopping . . . not caring what is under your boots, or how much noise you make. Not hearing the miniature wailing sounds as they recede behind you.

If animal trapped, call.

Following your steps back to the main lobby, you pass the emergency room. You don't stop to look at the bodies or their photo albums.

As you approach the front desk, something topples just behind you. There's a flash of movement to your left, jolting through your peripheral vision. Numbness washes out of you in a flood of panic. You raise the gun and pivot toward the noise.

A half-second slowly races by.

With a hollow, metallic crash, a large gray cat bursts from nowhere, scattering a pile of surgical trays. It scrambles past you, its tail brushing against your legs before it races down the hallway, disappearing into darkness.

Outside in the fading sunlight, you feel as though you've just left a trauma-therapy session.

You slip off your backpack and do a quick inventory of what you've got.

No more injuries, you say to yourself. *I don't like hospitals.*

Walking past the row of locked coroners' cars, you wonder about those vans you saw earlier. Would *they* have medical supplies? You've got to start taking better care of yourself: eating real food, for one thing, which will be hard—everything is rotted away.

Including the farmers, says your brain.

You *cannot* afford to become sick or injured. Never again. Not as long as things are like *this*. It cannot happen.

You look at the vans. Doors on most of them hang wide open—they're probably empty. You walk a quick perimeter of the main building, looking for anything else. On the far side of the parking lot, near a dumpster, you see what you were hoping for. A van labeled "Gracen Hospital" sits alone, its doors still shut.

You approach the derelict automobile, your gun in hand.

You check the cab: no driver, no passenger. You walk to the rear of the van, pause for a moment, and look through the double doors.

No one.

You see cabinets, though. They're closed, which means they might have something in them. Whatever it is, it needs to fit inside your backpack.

You grab the door handle and pull. It sticks. You give it a strong yank. And another—and that's when the car alarm starts blaring.

CHAPTER SIX

SURVIVING THE GRAVEYARD

MAKING THE BEST OF YOUR UNEMPLOYMENT

Boom! Head shot. *Boom!* Head shot.

Goddamned car alarms, you think, *how is that even possible? How had it not gone off already?*

You're backing up now, looking behind you while reaching into your pocket for another clip of ammunition.

Maybe the zombies set it, says your brain, *you know . . . for a gag.*

They just *descended* on you when the alarm sounded, coming out of nowhere, like bats from a cave.

Boom! Another scabbed-up, dripping ghoul meets an appropriately disgusting end, its head cracking apart like a morbid piñata. Whatever's inside isn't blood, and certainly isn't candy . . . it's black and lumpy. You wonder how their system even circulates it.

No point. No time.

You just start shooting and let your feet do the walking . . . to wherever you are now.

Boom! A clear miss. Dammit.

Your hand is still searching for that clip. Your hand is reporting back a big, fat nothing.

Come on . . .

Click.

It wasn't supposed to be this way. You were supposed to find someplace better to live, and hole up for as long as it took . . . eating, and relaxing, and . . .

Where the hell am I?

Your left hand continues to dig through your pockets; your right hand, still holding the gun, is patting down your clothing. The rest of you is wondering what part of the city this even *is* . . . nothing seems familiar.

You hear more scraping sounds. Not sure what direction they're coming from, you decide to skip right to the part where you sprint for home. Your backpack bounces as you accelerate: water bottles, a hatchet, supplies from the hospital, and some cans of food, all jostling for the chance to bruise you.

When you reach a small intersection, you pause to catch your breath. The stoplights are dead, of course. One of the metal frames tilts into the road, like a parody of those low-slung beach trees from a postcard.

You focus, and check your surroundings. To your right is a parking lot. To your left, a burned-out gas station. Across the street, each corner holds a building; one is a never-completed framework. The other is . . . full of people. Or what used to be people.

It's a pawnshop, the kind with bars on the windows and thick, steel mesh covering the door. The things inside move like sloweddown fish in a muddy tank. You're guessing they locked themselves in to be safe, and someone was infected. No one could find the key. Then everyone was infected.

There are at least thirty of them . . . bumping into one another, pushing mindlessly against walls, or just standing in place, rotting.

Time to go, your brain says.

You back up . . . slowly, carefully . . . then turn and jog down the street, accelerating as fear takes over. You imagine the houses on either side are filled with death, ready to pour out and flood the road.

Seeing a small group of lurching figures up ahead, you dart through a side street and scale a tall, wooden fence in little more than one jump. You land on the other side. Something slams into the fence behind you. You don't look back.

Ducking into a thick line of evergreen shrubs, you sling off your backpack and dig for the ammunition. Your hand closes on a clip.

You exhale, click the ammo into place, and glance back at the fence. It was a long drop—you landed on the downside of a steep hill.

Forward is the only option. You check your gun and step out into a large clearing, looking for the undead.

You don't have to look long. You see dozens of them . . . standing, limping . . . the ground seems to be covered with the crawling ones. Something that looks like a pile of trash with eyes is only a few feet away and pulling itself toward you. To your left, there's a hissing noise, and time seems to slow down. When it snaps back to normal, you're weaving your way through the clearing . . . clutching a pistol in your right hand while your left swings the hatchet like a club.

Some of the swings create thick, squishing sounds; an equal number hit what feel like dried-out branches.

Check the ground, check the ground, says your brain. There are so many half-bodies that it looks like you're being pursued by giant, angry water bugs.

Ahead, you see a massive willow tree; its trunk bisects about four feet up, splitting into a huge V shape and continuing its growth as two separate sections. You head straight toward it, and when you're within a few feet, you leap, aiming for the V.

Crashing into the space between the dual trunks, you don't wait to register the pain—you climb. You don't stop until the branches start to bend under your weight. You inspect the rest of the tree— below and above—several times before concluding that you're safe . . . sort of. Your lungs are hyperventilating in pitching, gasping gulps.

After you've regained your breath and control, you double-check that your pistol and backpack made it up with you. You're afraid to count your ammunition—whatever you've got is *all* you've got. Same for your water and your food.

You look out from the ad hoc perch. *Where are we?* asks your brain.

Squinting into the darkness, you see the outline of a low-level building, more trees, and a lot of ground-level shapes you can't make out.

They're not moving, whatever they are.

You stare a moment longer, your teeth grinding.

No . . . no . . . no . . . no . . . goddammit, NO.

They're the "stumps" you saw earlier.

You're back in the cemetery.

As darkness falls, you wonder how many bodies this graveyard holds.

Or used to.

No matter how hard you try, no matter what you do, there is always a chance that you will find yourself in the graveyard . . . you will be unemployed.

You can and will fight your way through this dark period. You will emerge on the other side—bloodied, perhaps, but unbowed.

Before we do anything else, however, let's take a moment. We're going to wallow.

Ready?

Yes, it sucks. A lot.

Your self-worth, your image in the eyes of friends or colleagues, the way you might think your spouse or partner sees you—these things take a beating every single day you're unemployed.* Your boss, your coworkers, your former employer—they still exist, in all likelihood. They're still around, just without you. For everyone else, nothing stops.

All those people who wish you well and who say they'll help out and do whatever they can? They're not lying, most of them. They mean it. And they will do what they can. *When* they can. When they're not working, or spending time with their spouse or partner, or taking a vacation. Because life goes on. *Your* life is your own, and it only keeps moving if you make it happen.

We're done with wallowing. It's time to get another source of ammunition. Take another moment, and let's begin.

---

* And if you think we're just giving lip service here—we're not. The authors of this book have been unemployed many times, for many different reasons . . . and usually without warning. Whatever the circumstances, the emotional/personal fallout—anxiety, stress, a sense of isolated gloom—is universal.

Increase Your Own Odds

Those things you've always heard about finding a job? They're true. Finding a job *is* your new job. It's also true that connections, favoritism, blind luck, and appearance make a difference. Keep in mind: This section is not about *why* such things matter; when the putrid, rotten horde is slowly massing below your cemetery tree house, "why" becomes a question for later.

This is a time for reality.

Here are the basics:

1. We'll say it again. Finding work is your new job.

   That means doing it every weekday, from nine a.m. until five p.m. Why? Because somebody, somewhere, is doing the same thing, and there aren't enough jobs for everyone. If that seems coldhearted, consider this: somebody, somewhere, is looking for work exactly *zero* hours a day . . . because his father owns the company, or his wife has connections with the hiring department, or a thousand other backroom, who-you-know machinations. You're competing with people who don't need any more advantages.

2. Set time limits on anything that takes away time during job-hunting hours. This includes television, reading,* and the Internet . . . especially the Internet. It's too easy to believe you're researching a new job or career when you're really ticking away minutes and seconds of your precious time.

3. Remember: When your conscience kicks in, it does so for a reason. More than just a barometer for right and wrong, it tells you when you're approaching danger—you ignore it at

---

* Yes, even *this* book.

your peril. It will tell you when you are spending too much time *pretending* to look for work and not enough time actually looking for work. It's easy to think that reading barista message boards counts as job-searching, but your conscience knows otherwise.

4. For generalized job searching (if you haven't settled on a particular field, or if your priority is to secure any paying job, period), trade publications offer little immediate benefit. They can, however, give you a sense of how companies *speak.* Business lingo changes with every era, but the particular tone that accompanies most "position available" listings is a near-constant.

5. When sending a résumé, interviewing for a job, or placing a "position sought" ad, speak to people the way *they speak.* Just as you should mirror an interviewer's posture and body language, emulating their verbal/written language is a way to increase a sense of connection. It makes strangers more comfortable and engaged with your presence, whether they know it or not.

How many zombies did I encounter today? Was it more than yesterday? Which gun is the best when exploring a small space? What stores have I already searched for supplies?

If you don't keep track, you forget. And then, you lose.

Below is a worksheet to track your job search. Think of these as a quick "calendar" on each potential job. You should keep additional notes, when necessary (contact names, connections, etc.), but this overview will help to keep you current, focused, and aware of your next move(s).

Job/Company	Date Job Posted	Date Applied	Interview Date	Follow-Up Sent

Job/Company	Date Job Posted	Date Applied	Interview Date	Follow-Up Sent
_____	_____	_____	_____	_____
_____	_____	_____	_____	_____
_____	_____	_____	_____	_____
_____	_____	_____	_____	_____
_____	_____	_____	_____	_____
_____	_____	_____	_____	_____
_____	_____	_____	_____	_____
_____	_____	_____	_____	_____
_____	_____	_____	_____	_____
_____	_____	_____	_____	_____
_____	_____	_____	_____	_____
_____	_____	_____	_____	_____

To the few people who have not gotten the memo:

Social networking sites are like giant, clear, sliding-glass doors in the walls of your fortress. If the wrong things are on display—a large food supply, for example, or those topless photos you took in Tahiti—you will draw trouble . . . and not *just* from zombies.

Everything you show the world through that window/website sends a message . . . sometimes the wrong message. Keeping your arsenal visible might repel looters, but it might also scare off potential rescuers. "Fun" photos become "inappropriate"; "edgy" becomes "unprofessional"; and "sassy" becomes "drama queen." As an added bonus, *you* go from "hired" to "devoured."

If you absolutely *must* post pages of snark/photos/rants for your drinking pals to snicker at, create a personal site that can *only* be accessed by people who have your permission and/or a password. (Though be warned that this, too, can raise red flags of the "What is he/she hiding?" variety.)

If you're looking for a specific career, don't be afraid to speak with others in your industry, and ask pointed questions about what they seek in a prospective employee. Don't *pretend* to be interested just to get your foot in the door—*be* interested and find real answers. Ask your questions directly, not as a passive-aggressive attempt to be hired.

Follow up these discussions (whether they happen in person or via phone, e-mail, etc.) with a brief note or e-mail thanking them for their time, and some variation on the phrase "Thanks again, and please let me know if I can ever be of assistance." Include complete contact information, send it . . . and forget it. Resist the urge to follow up unless you have a compelling reason to do so. They know you're looking for a job. Respect their time, and you'll maintain a positive association in their minds.*

When you do find work, always follow up with those who gave you advice, input, etc. If your new job is unrelated to their field, or if it's just something to pay the bills, omit the specifics but thank them for their time, and repeat the offer of future assistance.

Fighting Hand-to-Hand: The Interviewing Process

So there you are—you've managed to wangle an interview. This is your chance to close the deal. After all, of the myriad job applicants over any given week/month, a company rejects most of them, follows up with a few, and interviews only a handful. If you've made it this far, you owe it to yourself to give it all you've got.

Fight to survive . . . every single time.

The lesson here is simple: Overprepare. Here's how:

1. **Research the company.** Pore over their website, read coverage in trade magazines, scour news stories about recent activities and products, even look into which charities they may be involved with. You may be thinking that you'll never use most

---

* This is a good time to note that your public/professional e-mail address(es) should be as simple and professional as possible. Avoid dashes, underscores, or anything else that makes the address difficult to verbalize/remember. Try to include some or all of your name in the address, and resist the urge to be overly cute or clever; "deddhedd666" probably won't be the first one contacted for an opening.

of this information, and you'd be correct. What you're doing is taking every conceivable weapon into the fight. If given the opportunity, you want to know your territory, and you don't want to be surprised. You want them to be impressed by how much you've learned about the company. Will they know it's because you've crammed for this event? Most likely, but that's also in your favor: they want to hire the best person possible, and willingness to work above and beyond is worth its weight in gold.

2. **Rehearse your interviewing skills.** Make a list of questions you think you'll be asked. Make a separate list of what you'd *like* to be asked. Write answers for both. Your goal is to deliver this information without it sounding staged, forced, or contrived. Your first dozen attempts might be terrible, but those are just rehearsals. You will get better. As you practice, you might feel embarrassed or self-conscious. This feeling will vanish faster than you think, and once you've got the job, your rehearsal process will make for a great story.

3. **Know what you deserve.** When you are researching your industry, you should be able to easily find the salary range of people with jobs similar to the one you are looking for. Be prepared with this information if/when it enters the conversation.

HOW DO YOU FIND SALARY INFORMATION?

THE GOVERNMENT. The Bureau of Labor Statistics tracks wage estimates by location and occupation. Go to their site and look for "Occupational Employment and Wage Estimates" or "Occupational Employment Statistics" in the search window.

RELATED TO THE ABOVE: The Pentagon lists military salaries, and the Office of Personnel Management lists current pay for federal workers.

ONLINE JOB SITES. They sometimes provide salary information as a way to attract more people. Be sure to cross-check the info across more than one site; this will help assure that you're getting an accurate estimate.

After your interview, send a follow-up letter or e-mail thanking them for their time and interest. As with your note to people who answered questions about their industry, keep this message short, sweet, and polite, then move on to your next interview or prospect. Potential employers are much more concrete when giving good news than bad—if you've got the job, or if they want you to interview with someone higher up the ladder, they'll usually tell you. If, on the other hand, they've decided that you're not right for the job (for any number of reasons), they may not express it in those words. You may get a form letter, or a handwritten "Thank you for your interest, but . . ." message, or you may get nothing.

When you are passed over for a job—whether or not you receive an official "no"—do not relentlessly contact the employer, as you are likely to come off as needy, nagging, or desperate. These are not the words you want associated with your name in the mind of a potential employer.

In these cases, feeling disappointed is natural. Allow yourself a small moment of anger or annoyance, and then move on. There are nearly always more job seekers than jobs; rejection letters go out, phones remain silent, and qualified people sometimes don't get hired—it is the way of things.

Any Port in a Storm, Any Gun in a Swarm

When you have tons of ammunition, you use a machine gun. When your ammunition runs low, you swap down to a fifteen-shot pistol. When your clips are expended, you switch over to a pair of standard-issue revolvers—one in each hand, no waiting. You aim for the head, every time, with every shot. As your last remaining rounds click into place, you're firing and dropping the guns in one smooth motion. Your hand reaches back like an archer going for another arrow . . . and returns holding the crowbar that juts out of your backpack everywhere you go.

Swinging, ducking, your eyes scan for an opening . . . enough room to make a break for it. You keep hitting. You never stop. *You don't ever stop.*

As you continue your job search, as you angle for a position with career-building potential, or as you just look for something you won't flat-out despise, realize this: you might not have that choice.

Situations *do* improve, have no doubt. You've put yourself ahead of the game simply by being aware of the stakes. In the meantime, the zombies are swarming. They're sinking their teeth into your money, your peace of mind, and, if left unchecked, your future.

You will not let that happen.

When you don't have the weapon of your choice, you use the weapons you *do* have. When you have nothing at all, you find the nearest thing that makes a dent in zombie skulls. We're talking table legs . . . ax handles . . . or a job you never thought you'd be taking.

There is no job that is "beneath you." The only thing beneath you is giving up, giving in, and letting the undead flood your house. You are better than that.

Paychecks are ammunition. Maybe not enough to stop the zombie apocalypse, but that's a secondary priority. *Your* job is to survive. And every day you stay alive is a day you can spend looking for better weapons, more ammunition . . . a *better* job.

When a crowbar is all you have, you pick it up . . . and you swing with everything you've got.

What to Do Now

Earlier we discussed ways of cutting costs and maximizing every cent. Now it's time to get serious. This isn't forever . . . but if you don't do what is necessary for financial survival, it *could* be.

Turn off the television.

Silence your phone.

And let's make sure you have a future. Here are the steps:

1. **Apply for unemployment.** This is nonnegotiable. The money is there. It will continue to be there, whether you use it or not. If an asteroid hits you tomorrow morning, that money

vanishes back into the possession of the state. Reason enough to leave your job? Absolutely not. But definitely a reason to *use* that money when the time is right. Like . . . now.

You can register in person or online. Search "[your state] unemployment" and the first result should be the state's workforce/unemployment website. It should not be hard to sign up, but if it is, be relentless in calling and showing up in person to make sure you get it done. Take it seriously—it's a potential barrier between you and the gaping, gluttonous mouths outside.

Once you've registered, you'll receive additional information detailing—among other things—the total amount in your unemployment "fund." Pay close attention to this number. Divide it by the amount of your weekly benefit check (as noted in this same paperwork). The resulting number is the weeks remaining until your unemployment is gone.

Remember: The size of your unemployment fund is directly related to how much on-the-books work you've had in the previous year(s). Though extensions to your unemployment benefits are possible, once you're cut off (or your balance hits zero), you're done. Over. Finished . . . until you find a job and work long enough to build this fund back up.

2. **If you received a Severance Package,**[†] **put it in the bank untouched.** This is savings, period. Unless you are in dire circumstances—unless there is a zombie preparing to bite into your femur—this is ammunition to be stored. Again: unemployment benefits are for your absolute necessities. Severance is savings.

[†] **Severance Package** (*noun*): Money paid to an employee by an employer upon termination of said employment. Note: This term is becoming increasingly anachronistic.

3. **Continue to assess your expenses.** This will sound familiar, and it should: it's crucial. Cable/satellite TV, movie/video game rentals, restaurants, alcohol (in general, but specifically when purchased at bars), peak-time movie tickets, cell phone plans . . . everything needs to be addressed and scrutinized. Anything that is not necessary for living and finding a job is eligible for the chopping block. Resolve to eliminate two or three of these costs. Now.

The faster—and sooner—you make these decisions, the easier your route to survival.

Unemployed life is not like regular life, and while *you* may immediately recognize this, your friends may not. For myriad reasons, they may behave as though nothing has changed. *This cannot be allowed to damage your life.* Fifty dollars spent on drinks and appetizers is fifty dollars that could have fed you for a week and a half.

As corny as it sounds, true friends—and those who are not—will reveal themselves in times of crisis. When you suggest staying in with a movie or making dinner at someone's home, pay close attention to who stops calling . . . and who doesn't.

No one is coming to save you . . . but some may stay behind to help.

Six Shots to the Body

Below are basic steps toward slowing the zombies' approach. Taken as a whole, these shots can buy you valuable time.

1. **Get a roommate.** Or two. No matter what the overall economic picture is like, other people are facing the same situation you are, and roommates are a straightforward way to cut your rent, utility costs, sanitation costs, etc.

2. **You have things to sell.** Like everyone, you have a basement (or attic, or collection of boxes) filled with stuff you thought you'd use, but don't. Things you've probably forgotten all about. Sell this stuff. Do it online, but unless you're selling a truly big-ticket item, resist the pull of auction sites. These are swamps for time and energy, and often aren't worth the investment of either. Use Craigslist or a similar online service. If you'd rather take the hands-on approach, yard/garage sales are omnipresent for a reason: they work. Don't have the time (or the yard)? Find someone who will offer up the use of their yard/driveway and who, for the right cut of the profits, will run the sale for you. Even if you sacrifice 25 percent of the total take, that's 75 percent of money you wouldn't otherwise have.

3. **Maintain what you _do_ have.** Change the oil in your car (resist the full-service package; better yet, learn to change your own oil), empty the lint trap in your dryer, mend that little rip in your jeans. These sound like basic fixes, and they are: when the undead swarm your front porch, plugging a leaky water bottle is a major concern. Don't give the zombies any help.

4. **Skip the car.** Whenever possible, bike, walk, or use public transportation . . . it's possible more often than you think.

Learn the routes, learn the rates. Every time you board a bus/train/other, it minimizes wear and tear on your vehicle *and* instantly decreases your gasoline costs. And every time you bike or walk, you add "decrease my future medical bills" to the list.

5. **Face your vices.** Alcohol, soda, candy, cigarettes, drugs. All addictive. All dangerous. All expensive.

6. **Assess your abilities.** For every skill you have, there's someone who *doesn't* have it . . . or who doesn't have the time to use it. From the artistic (painting, assistance with redecoration) to the hands-on (lawn care, plumbing/electrical work) to the problem-solving (dog-walking, recipe/meal creation), look for opportunities to make money while staying flexible enough to continue your job search.

Keep Your Brain from Eating Itself: A Word on State of Mind

During any protracted period of stress, especially financial stress, it can sometimes feel as though things will never change—and that they might, in fact, get worse and worse. Progress feels scant, sometimes nonexistent. The light at the end of the tunnel, while real, can also be quite distant at times, and it's not always visible.

Things to keep you in the game:

1. **Keep close track of what you need to do:**

    Every night, without fail, make a list of your tasks, what you want and need to do the next day.

    Don't worry about having too many things on your list, just put down everything that needs to be done. Then, number them from 1 to 10 (or whatever the final number is) in terms of importance. Don't give more than one task the same number—you must decide what is most crucial for a given day.

The next day, as you move through the list, force yourself to go through the items in order. Trust that your nighttime self knew what it was doing.

If you can't accomplish a task, move down the list, but come back to it throughout the day until it's checked off. If necessary, move it to the next day's list, but keep it with you every day until you've done it.

2. **Make and keep a schedule.** This is especially important if you're **Underemployed**[†] or unemployed.

Every night, plan out your timeline for the following day. Who will you be contacting about a job? With whom are you following up? If your résumé or cover letter needs to be polished, schedule it.

Avoid doing this with sticky notes or random jottings on a tablet somewhere. Such random scrawls inevitably end up as crumples in your pocket, illegible and useless. Nor do you need to purchase bloated, expensive software that vows to organize your life.

The Internet offers a plethora of free schedulers, task-tracking tools, and calendars—often as an adjunct to an online e-mail account. If push comes to shove, spend no more than five dollars on a pocket calendar—but get a system, and stick with it. You must ingrain your behaviors or they'll never last, and you'll slide back into apathy and disarray.

If you have recurring scheduled events (playing a team

---

† **Underemployed** (*adjective*): Employed to such a degree that one may not receive jobless benefits via the government, yet employed to an insufficient degree to allow for the payment of living expenses.

sport, a monthly lunch with a friend, a novel you're writing), stick to your schedule. Your brain needs structure, and when your brain feels like things are happening—when it feels active, productive, useful—it will respond accordingly. It will stay switched on and busily crank out ideas and suggestions . . . many of them massively helpful when it comes to getting out of this mess.

3. **Dress for how you want to feel.** If you want a shortcut to feeling helpless, here's a hint: Don't shave in the morning. Don't shower, brush your hair, or put on anything resembling clean pants. Dress like a victim. Walk out onto the porch and announce your willingness to be torn into screaming shreds.

    Or dress like someone with a purpose. Dress like someone who is refusing to back down. This will drastically impact your outlook, your focus, and your productivity.*

4. **Be cautious about your alcohol and/or drug intake.**

    Filling yourself with chicken strips and tequila may be temporarily satisfying, but it will lower your energy levels, make you generally sluggish, and ultimately remove what your body needs to move forward and maintain its focus.

    We're not lecturing, but just as alcohol makes someone who is freezing to death feel warmer (while it's actually lowering their body temperature), drugs and drinking can instill a deceptive sensation of calm or well-being, which can turn into a depressed hangover . . . or worse, a spiraling cycle of lift and crash. And drugs cost money. Lots of money.

---

* It will also spare you this horrifying moment: A prospective employer calls, asking if you can meet her downtown in forty-five minutes . . . which is when you realize you're wearing wrinkled jeans and a stained concert tee, you haven't showered, and you have no time to iron.

5. **Read.** Reading activates different sections of your brain than visually based activities such as television or video games. In addition to keeping your brain sharp and alert, reading is a sort of mental vacation that other forms of entertainment simply can't match: studies show that reading lowers blood pressure and activates/magnifies feelings of calm and focus.

Finally, reading activates the left side of your brain, which is the part that helps you make critical decisions and weigh risks/benefits. This side of your brain also deals with numbers, calculations, and linear thinking—all of them crucial skills when it comes to your survival.

Feed your brain . . . or feed it to the zombies. The choice is up to you.

Researchers at the University of Sussex found that as little as six minutes of reading can reduce stress levels by more than two-thirds. Seriously.

6. **Exercise.** It's cheap, it's simple (if not always easy), and it will help keep you out of the hospital.

Need more motivation? You'll lose weight.

Need more? What they say about endorphins is true—when you're done with a regular workout, you'll feel better, both physically and mentally. And let's not beat around the bush: when you're in shape (or getting in shape), others will notice. They'll comment. You'll feel like a million bucks.

Or you can be another spongy, bloated mess at the food court . . . slurping from a plastic tankard and waiting for the zombies. Your choice.

We won't lie: you may hate exercising . . . but you'll love having exercised.

7. **Ask for help.** Fear and stress are natural responses to difficult situations. They're what kept our ancestors alive—and they're what will help keep you from making your own challenges worse.

There may come a time, however, when you feel exhausted and incapable of making rational decisions. You might consider drastic, unhealthy measures in response to your circumstances. If you should find yourself in this state of mind, do not hesitate to seek help. This doesn't necessarily mean you need treatment or medication. While such things can be helpful for any number of reasons, it can be just as useful to simply find an outlet for your stress. Your local/community/state mental health and counseling centers are trained to deal with a vast spectrum of problems and issues, from the common to the unique. Judge the situation. Reach out for professional help or just call a friend, whatever fits your need.

Most of all, you are absolutely forbidden to feel weak or guilty about seeking such help. Your brain and body are the only real assets you have—everything else flows from these two resources. If something is amiss with either your physical or your mental well-being (even if it's as seemingly minor as needing to vent), there are places and people who can help, and can do so without any serious impact to your budget . . . sometimes completely without cost.

At ZombieEconomics.com, you will find a list of resources available by state and region. These services operate confidentially, and most are available twenty-four hours a day.

8. **Avoid people with a Death Wish.**[†] You know the type: complains about their job, their boss, their family, their money, their unemployment, their roommate, their now empty unemployment fund, and, and, and, and.

 Bad things happen . . . we all know it. We all get it. Now move on.

 "Friends" who dwell on dark, negative, bitter experiences or emotions are dangerous in multiple ways. Acknowledging reality is one thing, but there's no point in fighting yesterday's battles over and over again. People who stare into the rearview mirror will have exactly the same scenery a year from now. Move forward . . . even if it must be without them.

 Also: Spend time with people you want to be like. This doesn't necessarily mean "spend time with a gaggle of wealthy bankers"; it means finding those whose personality traits mirror those you'd like to see in yourself. It can also mean spending time with people who bring out the better elements of your nature. Everyone faces adversity; seeing how others have survived—and retained their sense of self—is of infinite value. It also has a positive impact on your own state of mind to be with people who are facing things realistically, honestly . . . without attaching needless negativity.

9. **Blame the victim, but don't be the victim.** As the saying goes, there are only two kinds of actions: what life does to you, and what you do back. When things turn bad, some people seem determined to make the situation even worse; they make incredibly poor choices, even after recognizing their behavior.

 You will not be one of these people.

---

† **Death Wish** (*noun*): A compulsion to dwell upon, relive, and, in some cases, draw inexplicable pleasure from perceived or genuine personal hardship. See also: *Drama queen.*

Don't let past choices continue to take a toll on your well-being and your life. Use them as stepping-stones to a different way of behavior. We're not claiming that you'll become a shrewd financial operative overnight, but we can guarantee that using your past experience as an object lesson puts you leagues ahead of most other people. By consciously avoiding bad planning, by vowing not to retread the same shaky ground over and over again, you have already increased your own odds.

PERIODS OF UNEMPLOYMENT can be very difficult to endure—anyone who says differently is lying. But they are, at their core, made up of moments. As hard as it might initially be, remember that *this is only temporary.*

When depression threatens to overtake you—when the tunnel's light seems a hundred miles away and obscured by gloom—remember that you didn't come this far to give up now.

Visualize your life story as a book, and these challenging times as the early chapters, when the hero is facing adversity.

You are the hero. Really.

How long is a day, anyway?

Twenty-four hours? Maybe . . . if you're operating under conventional circumstances. If you're rested, and well-fed, and hydrated. Maybe . . . if you get some sleep and some kind of tentative, shaky security . . . a day might pass in twenty-four hours.

In a tree, in a cemetery, with dead human beings walking the landscape in every direction, their flesh decayed and molding, filling the air with a smell like the inside of a coffin . . .

That makes all the difference in the world.

According to your wristwatch, you've been up here for three days. According to the sun, you've been up here for three days.

Your brain and your stomach—they've got a different take on things.

Your stomach keeps waiting for sundown, thinking that darkness will allow some kind of escape . . . some way to climb down and slip past the corpses dotting the cemetery lawn like horrible Halloween exhibits.

Also, your brain reminds you helpfully, *sundown means less heat, which means . . .*

. . . which means less sweat, you finish, and you can feel the thick, sticky slowness in every swallow, like the insides of your mouth and windpipe have been smeared with peanut butter.

All things considered, time is passing a little *too* quickly. At this rate, three days will become four, then five, then . . .

Then we become a permanent fixture in this tree, your brain says, *like a tangled kite . . . only skinnier.*

If you're still here in forty-eight hours, your body, dehydrated to begin with—the result of a panicked, adrenaline-filled sprint down the street, followed by another frantic burst of energy to reach the tree—will begin turning off nonessential functions to save itself. Little things like balance . . . or the ability to speak. Slowly, those nonessential functions will be shut off *permanently,* followed by more important things . . . like breathing, and regulating your heart-beat. Then there won't be any more heartbeat.

Dying in a cemetery is just weird, your brain says.

For the thousandth time, you stare toward the south end of the cemetery lawn. At least, you *think* it's the end of the lawn; there's no way to be sure. About half a mile from your vantage point, the grass slopes down and out of sight. Past that, there's a large swath of trees, thick and overlapping, spreading out for hundreds of yards, side to side. The distance, the trees, and the downward curve of the grass all combine to create a huge shadowed area. No matter the time, no matter how hard you look, you can't get any kind of a fix on what might be in there.

Could be a fence . . . or a wall. Could be more tombstones. Could be a small forest . . . or a park . . . or some different, smaller part of the graveyard . . . like a family plot . . . or . . .

Does it matter? your brain finally interrupts.

You can't say that it does. Not at this point.

Your eyes aching with exhaustion and frustration, you check your supplies. Your pistols are loaded and ready, but you're low on ammunition. You'll keep one tucked in your belt. Your left hand will clutch the hatchet—blade facing inward, so you can swing it like a bludgeon. Anyway, if you fall, the blade will be the least of your worries.

You jiggle your last water bottle. All but empty.

Let's go, says your brain. W*e might not get another chance.*

It takes another twenty-five minutes of watching and waiting before the revolting, carnivorous figures on the cemetery lawn are in an acceptable arrangement. Like a chess player, you're looking at the whole picture, not just individual pieces. You think you spot a winding path through the maze of teeth and claws.

Knowing the opening won't last long, you toss the pistol to the ground, swing the lower half of your body down off the branch, and drop, landing with a soft thud. You grab the gun, look toward the dark area beneath the southward trees, and start moving.

Some thirty yards to your right, a zombie moans . . . and decaying, maggot-filled heads turn in your direction. Within seconds, they're starting to converge, like filth circling a bathroom drain.

You club the first two, and then something's got your right foot, digging into your boot. You're swinging as you turn, the hatchet coming down.

It's a sprinkler head. You twist to avoid hitting yourself with the hatchet's blunt end. You stumble. You fall to the ground. A zombie looms into focus overhead, making strangled, high-pitched noises. It's got no mouth at all—everything below the eyes has been torn out, leaving a giant, wet cavern. It's coming down at you face-first, squealing. You jam the gun straight up and pull the trigger. The head explodes into a shower of rotten pieces. You yank your foot free and get moving.

You cross another twenty yards. Another fifty.

You're almost there.

You pass armless, legless, scrabbling things, their moldy voice boxes turning everything into a wet, drowning gasp.

Almost there.

Just outside the stand of trees, something that used to be a little girl is tangled in a mass of branches, flailing, its mouth snapping like a turtle's. As you draw closer, it lunges, fixing on you with open, empty eye sockets, clawing at the air. The undergrowth holds it in place; a moment later, your hatchet ends its manic, tearing convulsions.

Looking closer, you see why it couldn't move: it was caught in a teeming snarl of blackberry vines. Like everything else, they've grown out of control; some seem as thick as your wrist. There is no fence to the south . . . the blackberry brambles *are* the fence.

Things unspool in slow motion as you turn and look back into the cemetery. There are at least three dozen zombies coming directly at you; even the sluggish, decayed ones are closing in. Escaping back the way you came—across the lawn—is impossible. You wonder if that's what brought the little girl this way . . .

. . . back when she was still a little girl.

The next moment, you're hacking at the vines with your hatchet. The blade seems puny, feeble, barely making a dent. There are just too many, and they're too thick. You don't bother looking behind you before deciding to simply climb.

Your hands grab what feel like fistfuls of biting wasps, and you pull yourself up—first your right leg, then your left. The good news is that the thorns and jagged vine ends hook directly into the front of your jeans . . . of course, that's also the bad news. The dusty, needle-sharp points are puncturing your fingers and the palms of your hands. You grit your teeth, trying to block out the pain, trying to think of something else.

If someone's up here . . . if someone got bitten, and then crawled up here and got stuck . . .

Let's stop thinking of other things, your brain interrupts. *Let's just climb.*

Fighting your way up the brambles, you ignore the ongoing perforation of your legs and the feeling that you are burrowing into the belly of some massive, thorny creature.

Suddenly, there's nothing underneath you. Your stomach rises as you plummet. Half a second later, you're on the ground, feeling as though you've hit solid concrete. In fact, you have.

Barely aware that you are making listless moaning noises of your own, you get on your feet and limp down the alley, fingers clutching at a pistol. Adrenalized beyond the point of pain, you don't feel the deep, inch-long scratches covering your body; you've forgotten about the injuries to your bandaged left arm.

You lurch forward, one step at a time, never stopping; never looking back.

Hundreds of staggered steps later, traveling down a little-used back road, your surroundings start to feel strangely familiar; half-formed connections in your head produce what seem like visual echoes.

You're nearly there before you figure it out.

Your parents' home is straight ahead.

Even from thirty yards away, you can see the blood on the windows.

CHAPTER SEVEN

SHOOTING DAD
IN THE HEAD

ENDING YOUR RELATIONSHIPS WITH
THE FINANCIALLY INFECTED

Warring impulses fight for control of your movements: half of you wants to run toward your parents' house at full speed; the other half is calm, detached . . . already preparing for the worst. You move forward as though on a conveyor belt—barely aware of your own footsteps. Even less aware of the blood soaking through your pants and shirt.

Arriving at the front porch, you look through the large window next to the door, hoping that you've gotten it wrong somehow . . . looking for another family's pictures on the wall.

Nope. There you are. And there, in the same photo, your sister, father, and mother. Everyone trying to look like the best versions of themselves. Hair sprayed, eyeglasses carefully adjusted, smiles that say, Boy, this photographer has no idea what he's doing. Do I have to sneeze? Am I showing too many teeth? Do I—

Click.

Your family, as it existed on that day, seven years ago. It was actually kind of great.

You fall out of the memory, and you're back on the porch. There are burn marks by your feet—from what, you don't know. Some broken glass. A few bullet casings. The screen door is in place, but torn from the hinges; it's just leaning into the frame. The front door is slightly ajar; the lock seems to have been chiseled right out of the knob.

You're distantly aware of your thirst and hunger, but you stand for several minutes, immobile. The sun beats down; the air is hot and still. A small corner of your mind wonders how the rest of the food chain is faring these days. It's been a while since you've seen anything bigger than a squirrel. You're guessing whatever could burrow went as deep as it could, and whatever could fly went as high as wind and physics would take it. As for the rest, you've seen a few large packs of dogs . . . many of them still wearing their tags and collars; all of them staring at you with glinting, unflinching eyes. They don't appear to be infected. And they look very well fed.

Meanwhile, you're still on the front porch, inches from the door, wondering what you'll find inside. Finally, your brain pipes up in a nervous voice. *Look . . . uh . . . there's probably nothing to worry about here . . . the place seems pretty deserted.*

You're thinking the same thing, and not sure how to feel about it.

But you know, your brain continues, *there's a good chance they left some food and water down in the basement.*

Your parents believed in planning for emergencies, and while the current situation might not call for road salt or a poncho, if no one else has discovered the boxes and bottles downstairs . . .

As if on cue, your thirst and hunger reannounce themselves. Your legs feel weak from days and days of running. Of hiding. Of sleeping so little that things have taken on a haze of unreality. You have to get something in your stomach. And you need water. You can't wait much longer.

You set the screen door aside, and, using the pistol, you nudge the front door open. Stepping over the threshold, you see almost nothing but clothing and paper and dishes and dirt. It's like a combination homeless camp and clearance sale.

You realize that everything you see has been picked over by a series of looters, animals, and God-knows-what else.

There's no way there's anything left in the basement, you think, but your feet keep moving.

In the kitchen, every single cupboard is open and empty, but this doesn't surprise you . . . they would have moved everything down-stairs. You try the sink's faucet. Nothing happens, of course.

Out of habit, you turn toward the refrigerator and see letters on the wall, eight inches high stretching from floor to ceiling:

We have gone to Marshall Hospital. Try to find us there.

Don't stay in the house. The door won't hold very long.

It looks like your mother's handwriting, but you can't be sure. One thing you do know: Marshall Hospital burned down weeks ago—you could see the flames for miles.

You turn around, heading for the basement. *I wonder when the door gave out,* you think, remembering the chiseled lock and torn hinges on the front porch.

You hold the pistol at chest level as you walk down the hallway. You block out memories of what these rooms used to be. No one lives here anymore.

At the basement door, you stop and take a breath, preparing yourself for whatever is down there.

You hear it before you see it. A guttural, rotted drone—somewhere to your right. Before you can react, another noise erupts . . . a loud, splintering crash.

It's in your old bedroom, breaking through what remains of the door—just a couple of wooden slats nailed across the frame. It's ramming into the boards headfirst, arms lunging out, clawing. The stench is unbearable . . . sweet and rotten, like the bottom of a trash can.

Don't stay in the house. The door won't hold very long.

The creature slams into the boards over and over—staggering back, then driving forward. Staggering back, then driving forward.

Why didn't they kill it?

Your brain answers in a small, thin voice.

Because they couldn't.

Why couldn't—?

Let's go.

Another crash.

Let's go. Let's go. Let's go let's go let's go—

A decayed, bubbling moan fills the air, and the other voice is suddenly gone. It's just you . . . and the cracking, breaking boards . . . and a horrible thing dressed up as your father.

Don't stay in the house. The door won't hold very long.

This will not be easy. No one (well, almost no one) wakes up in the morning hoping to terminate—or at least seriously strain—a friendship before nightfall. No one wants to tell an irresponsible parent that the time has come to sever the financial harness. And absolutely no one relishes the prospect of giving a fiscal ultimatum to their bedmate.

This will not be easy.

For certain readers, however, it will be crucial. For others, it will be important. For the rest, it will be, at minimum, a valuable warning.

IF THE ZOMBIE ECONOMY has infected a friend or loved one, you probably know. Just as surely as with drugs or alcohol, you know when you are witnessing dangerous, irresponsible behavior with money.

Because we're good sports, we'll take a moment to lay out the symptoms:

ARE YOU FRIENDS WITH A FINANCIAL ZOMBIE?

Watch for the signs:

- Do they routinely use payday-advance or check-cashing services (or other **Predatory Lenders**)? [†]
- Do they seem to be continually shopping, buying the

[†] **Predatory Lenders** (*noun*): Any entity (usually a legal, licensed business entity) that lends monies at exorbitant interest rates, or with draconian penalties for late payment. Often shields its employees behind bulletproof glass . . . for any number of reasons.

latest phone, gadget, clothes, accessories, etc., when they clearly can't afford it?

- Is shopping their central social activity—the primary way they spend time with friends? Do they shop to relieve stress?
- Do they ask to borrow money in nonemergency situations? Repeatedly?
- Do they joke—even brag—about their precarious financial state? Do they use flip, cutesy phrases such as "retail therapy"?
- Do they buy gifts—often expensive gifts—for every imaginable occasion, despite their own financial instability?
- Have they used questionable/delusional financing to purchase a house/condo they obviously cannot afford?

Spot the symptoms . . . before it's too late.

Rent-to-own agreements, constant upgrades to their home electronics, the sudden appearance of sport or recreational vehicles, jewelry, expensive vacations . . . you get the picture. And you should be insulted. You ought to take personal offense at those who offer themselves up to be consumed like steaks on a platter.

You will use them as examples of how not to live your financial life. You will realize their mistakes, and you will vow not to replicate them.

And you will make certain that these friends, these loved ones . . . do not infect you.

SO HOW DO you stay safe from your own inner circle? Isn't that a little like staying dry (and safe) in a hurricane? The truth is, it's like anything else. You have to be determined and take specific steps to make sure any nearby financial illness ends before it infects you.

Protect Yourself

- Do not cosign a loan . . . for anybody. No one is served by putting two people on the hook for one loan. Not the bank, which may never earn back its investment; not you, who doesn't have the money to cover your friend's potential debts (if you did, he'd be asking you for the money); and not your friend, who is already a bad risk for the money, as evidenced by the fact that he needs a cosigner. When you lend money, you risk the money and your friendship. When you cosign a loan, you risk friendship, money . . . and your own good name and credit.

- Unless someone is a member of your immediate family and living under the same roof as you, do not add the person to your cell phone plan or any similar contract, period.

- Never add anyone else's debt to your credit card, even if you have a better APR (lower interest rate) than they do. If you take on someone else's debt, it becomes your debt to answer for, and it will directly affect your **Credit Score**.†

- Do not put up collateral for any type of financial agreement made by another person.

- Do not lend money to friends. That said, if you feel like you absolutely must assist and that the friend is "good for it," then you should test the waters by loaning a small amount. This should be accompanied by a clearly stated written agreement specifying how and when this money will be paid back. How

---

† **Credit Score** (*noun*): A numerical representation of a person's perceived credit-worthiness. This score is determined by three credit-ranking organizations and has an almost-other-worldly impact on your life and purchasing ability.

they treat this small loan is a strong indicator of how they will treat a larger one.

- Do not let a financially irresponsible friend or family member move in with you. Take it from us: they will stay longer than anticipated—certainly longer than you were told—and there's a good chance they'll never leave at all. If you are in an apartment, you may end up moving out to resolve the situation.

- Do not let a financially irresponsible (or generally irresponsible) friend or family member borrow your car. If someone lacks a license or insurance, is legally prohibited from driving, or has a track record of accidents, do not allow them to use your car. If they have been ticketed even once for driving while impaired, do not allow them to use your car under any circumstances.*

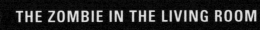

THE ZOMBIE IN THE LIVING ROOM

For some of you, it may be too late to keep the undead intruder from your home. This abomination may, even now, be sitting in a nearby armchair, rotting away—TV clicker in one hand, a fistful of bad credit in the other.

If the danger has breached the walls of your house, apartment, condo, or relationship, you cannot delay. You must take action now . . . or wake up dead.

- Do you share a joint bank account with a **Zombie Spouse**†/ or significant other? You are strongly urged

---

* Note: The "short-term" guest who stays for three months will inevitably want to borrow your car.

† **Zombie Spouse** (*noun*): Romantic partner with whom you physically share a home and belongings, yet whose presence in your home and life actually saps you of money, resources, and financial strength. A partner who does not share your fiscal rules or beliefs, especially those relating to self-discipline or frugality.

to set up a separate account that has no connection to them whatsoever. Remember: The bank, lender, etc., can be instructed to alert you if a payment is missed. This may help to reduce/eliminate penalty fees. Learn how your spouse's finances could impact your credit score. And remember: When applying for a loan, a lender will consider both credit scores . . . yours and your zombie spouse's.

- Have you made the mistake of cosigning a loan, or offering your money or belongings as collateral for another person? Seek the counsel of a lawyer. This will maximize your odds of escaping the situation (if possible). Your lawyer will also assist with the navigation of loopholes, footnotes, and fine print; in the long run, this will save you time, trouble, and possibly money.

- Are you connected to a zombie via an ongoing contract (such as a cell phone plan)? You are advised to break the contract and get out, even if it means incurring a penalty. This penalty pales in comparison to the long-term suffering (and financial loss) that come with being lashed to a zombie.

- Are you living with—but not married to—a zombie? Do you wish to separate the financial relationship while staying together? Do not hesitate to spell out—in explicit detail—the specifics of the financial arrangement: what will be shared, what will (and will not) be commingled, division of payment responsibilities, etc.*

---

* While this is solid, practical advice, we're not lawyers, and laws may differ wildly from state to state. Consult with an attorney and/or an accountant before making any drastic financial decisions.

Are you merely cohabitating with a zombie? Perhaps a roommate? A college friend? Some guy who was just there when you moved in? Consider the simplest solution: moving out. Speak with your landlord, explain the situation, and discuss your options. If moving is both necessary and viable, inform the zombie of your intentions, set a date, and leave. If you incur penalties for moving out, pay them . . . and chalk them up to the cost of your own survival.

Remember: You may spot your friend or loved one's infection before they do. It is vitally important that you be alert to their symptoms and behavior—it's the only way to be safe.

Pull the Trigger

This will not be easy.

Fortunately, it won't be necessary in most situations. Most people do, after all, have their own best interests at heart—they listen to reason, and they learn to avoid dangerous or destructive choices.

Some people don't, however, and that's when the zombies come. And the person you love—be it friend, parent, spouse, child—is finally overtaken by the very doom they tempted. And then it's too late. They've joined the zombies. Their behaviors will never change . . . and they will, inevitably, endanger you.

When this happens, there is only one solution. It is stressful, depressing, and often difficult to explain to others . . . but it is absolutely crucial.

It means aiming for the head.

It means zero tolerance. It means refusing to loan money to a desperate, irresponsible relative. It means forgoing social time with a friend whose spending habits are out of control. It means letting a loved one lose a car to repossession . . . a car they couldn't afford in the first place. It means cutting off the disease. It means saying no.

"But she's my best friend . . . she's always been there for me."

"Uncle Steve was always my favorite. I can help him . . . it's the least I can do."

"But it's my dad."

We'll say this once, and once only:

You are not responsible for the behavior of the infected. You are not obligated to "fix" their problems, and even if you were, it wouldn't matter . . . because you can't. You cannot change, control, or mend someone else. Not with drinking, not with drugs, not with overspending. And if you think we're being overdramatic, remember: There are numerous studies that correlate compulsive, irresponsible financial behavior with overeating, alcoholism, drug abuse, and other self-destructive addictions.

You cannot cure a financial zombie.

You can sympathize, you can offer tangible, practical suggestions, or point them toward organizations that assist with serious financial/behavioral issues. But you cannot cure them, so don't try. If you do, it will cost you. In every way you can imagine.

Always know this: When you pull the trigger, the target isn't your uncle, or your dad, or your best friend—it's the disease. A disease that knows no loyalties or boundaries.

When the disease comes in the form of a loved one, doing what is necessary becomes even more difficult. We're wired for empathy, for caring. That's what allows the infection to spread.

Remember this: There is no good that comes from both of you being bankrupt or desperate.

Remember this: You cannot cure a zombie.

Remember this: You cannot fix another human being.

Remember this: Survive.

WHEN YOU PULL the trigger—when you tell a friend, partner, or relative that you will no longer aid their financial infection—their reaction might surprise you. They may feign understanding, even agreement. Their mouth may say all the right things, but you are hearing a disease attempt to worm its way back into your house. The Zombie Economy thrives on contact—without new victims, it stalls out and dies off. Just as cocaine makes its victims beg, and cry, and bargain; just as alcohol turns its abusers into charming, amiable folks who just need "one more chance."

Other financial zombies may react differently. Some will turn bitter and angry at these new ground rules. You may be accused of false friendship, of not caring, of being "out of touch," and of the old standby: selfishness.

Don't fight. There's no point. You're not dealing with a person, just a disease with a human voice.

When the dust has cleared, gauge their behavior. Do they eventually change their ways? Do they exhibit a true understanding of why you made such a difficult, devastating decision? How they behave (and how they treat you) in the weeks and months afterward will speak volumes: Do they truly view you as a friend, or as another (former) enabler? Do they care about you, or are you just one more wallet in their girls-night-out, free-spending horde? Mom said it best: If they cut you off emotionally because of your refusal to be an economic crutch, then they weren't your friend to begin with.

IF YOU'RE STILL HESITATING

More reasons to make a break or pull back:

1. When you're around people who spend too much, you will spend too much. There is nothing surprising or shameful about this—it's simply human nature. Proximity breeds similarity—in ways both good and bad.

2. Enabling your friends and family—whether by loaning them money, ignoring their harmful decisions, or passively tolerating their dangerous spending habits—will take an inevitable toll on you, both mentally and financially.

3. Keeping up with the Joneses is incredibly appealing, but eventually deadly. No one can dispute the awesomeness of a three-hundred-inch television, but when the repo man hauls away your expensive, ultimately useless crap, trust us: it will seem a lot less awesome. Surrounding yourself with people who compulsively spend—and overspend—will lead to only one place: a McMansion you can't afford filled with **Zombie Bait**[†] you don't use. All of it on credit cards. Your financial life . . . over.

4. This isn't just a matter of good advice or good behavior. In most states it is a matter of law when

---

† **Zombie Bait** (*noun*): An item purchased—often impulsively—by a consumer, despite the consumer's awareness that the item far exceeds what the consumer can afford. These items are typically purchased for unsound, often self-deceptive reasons, and are often bright and/ or shiny.

you are financially involved with someone else. Your bank account, your home, your car, your possessions—all of this is on the table, and it all can be taken away. You are just not equipped to be a monetary savior for those around you. If you are a parent, you want to make sure you have money stored away for your kids in the event of a **True Emergency**.[†] These are usually (and hopefully) once-in-a-lifetime scenarios you will not be able to address if you've pissed away your savings on someone else's avoidable problems.

Breaking the News

We'll keep saying it, because it will always be true: This will not be easy. Making a financial separation is difficult. Severing an emotional/friendship connection is painful. Combine the two? It becomes harder than anything you might have imagined. The only thing harder will be doing nothing. Waiting, delaying, and, inevitably, suffering through the same infection that's destroying their existence, unable to help even if you wanted to—both of you struck down by an opportunistic financial monster that takes any opening it finds.

[†] **True Emergency** (*noun*): An urgent situation threatening death, serious bodily harm, mental trauma, or loss of freedom. While parents may understandably view any number of situations involving their children as True Emergencies, it's worth noting that car repossession is worlds apart from, say, needing to be bailed out of a Salvadoran prison.

WHAT ABOUT QUARANTINE?

You may be asking yourself, Why a head shot? Why not just stick them in the basement . . . or board them up inside the bedroom? Why not just distance myself from a financially destructive person . . . avoid being caught up in their behaviors?

These approaches could all potentially backfire. **Quarantine,**[†] after all, doesn't kill the zombie, and may not stop the disease's spread; it reduces the risk, but doesn't eliminate it. One broken hinge, one rotten door frame, one bad loan, and you're right back in the thick of things . . . and you may not get a second chance. The zombie will always need more help, will always need another loan, will always need someone else's noninfected name to make a purchase . . . it is inevitable.

Our advice? Quarantine will kill you. Address the problem now, before it costs you everything.

---

† **Quarantine** (*verb*): To isolate the diseased or infected in an effort to protect oneself from infection. Often used by the friends or relatives of a financial zombie despite the technique's overwhelming failure rate.

You understand why they couldn't kill him.

Crash.

Your father, on a cold February morning, teaching you how to ride without training wheels.

Creak. The door frame squeals and whines; nails twisting out of holes.

Your father's hands, strong and steady, bandaging your knee after your first spill off the bike.

Crash. You hear teeth grinding and clicking. The thing backs up, hits the door. Backs up, hits the door. Over and over and over.

The look of pride on his face when you graduated.

I can save him.

No. Your brain, in a stronger voice now. *No . . . you can't.*

He's just . . . I can just—

He's gone, your brain says, as the door's topmost board finally breaks, leaving two more.

Then you see the face. Scratched, unblinking eyes. Large divots of missing flesh where the planks have gouged it out like rancid ice cream.

You see blood around the mouth. It's not his own, you realize with a dull, insulated pain.

Your thoughts trail off and then, suddenly, you're moving through the house. Your brain is steering you toward your father's study, your body on autopilot.

Food and water, your brain says, leaving no room for argument, *we need food and we need water.*

Entering the office, you pass your father's desk . . . glass and dried blood covering the surface.

But first . . .

You're kneeling, your hands rummaging through the bottom of a large, crowded bookcase, finally pulling out the fronts of three false volumes. Reaching back into the jumble of books, your fingers touch plastic. You pull out a box of ammunition, then another. A quick feel says there are at least three more. You fill your backpack until the hiding place is empty. You load your pistol, then hesitate.

Down to the basement. Get some water. Get some food. Then . . . go.

You dash across the office and out into the hallway. And then you stop.

A monster made from children's nightmares is standing in your way.

You feel the weight of the gun in your hand.

Go, says your brain.

Run, says your brain.

Kill it, says your brain.

For the longest half-second of your life, nothing happens.

You think of the picture on the living room wall.

You open your mouth to say goodbye, and the monster comes right at you, howling through a mass of snapped-off teeth.

In one motion, you raise the gun, fix on the monster's face, and pull the trigger.

The boom goes down the hallway.

There's a thud.

The floorboards creak.

There is no other sound.

You look down, and fire two more shots.

They echo out.

This isn't your father. This is a disease.

You step over the monster's stinking remains and open the basement door.

When you emerge minutes later, you've got a backpack bulging
with water bottles, freeze-dried food, and several more boxes of
ammunition. For good measure, you've stuffed a smaller, empty
knapsack inside your shirt.

You force your attention straight ahead, stepping over the immobile creature and walking toward the front door. It's time to get
back home. To *your* home.

When you're safely bolted inside your small, cramped, beautiful,
fortified house . . . then you can start thinking about how to locate
your mother and sister.

We have gone to Marshall Hospital. Try to find us there.

"I'll find you," you say in a quiet voice.

CHAPTER EIGHT

THE TRENCH

FINANCIAL DEFENSES THAT
WORK WHILE YOU SLEEP

The harrowing chain of experiences—beginning with your inadvertent discovery of the cemetery, and ending with the nightmarish events at your parents' home—has brought into razor-sharp focus the need to stay in a secure environment. Upon returning to your own house (mercifully, it was not looted or destroyed), you decide to preemptively quell any bouts of cabin fever—you don't imagine you'd be quite so lucky next time.

First comes extra security: layers of blankets and clothing go up over the windows, held in place by a few long nails you manage to pull out of the frame.

Then, little by little, comes comfort—the slow, careful process of making your house more livable. This is about staying inside and still keeping your sanity. This is about making your home a fortress, not a prison.

Very gradually, you add things: a different chair, some brand-new bedding you found. Function over form; enjoyment over aesthetic. Anything that wasn't useful didn't come home, no matter the brand, no matter how much it might have cost . . . before. These new items share space with the most important acquisition of all: books. Hundreds and hundreds of books.

The doors are blocked, the windows are boarded, and every piece of ammo you find goes directly into storage.

Now, there's only one way to make the house even safer—keep the goddamned zombies from getting to it in the first place.

A trench? your brain asks.

A trench, you respond, checking the index of a military encyclopedia.

And who's going to dig it?

You ignore the question and continue reading. You're looking for information on small-scale conflicts and uprisings. On guerrilla warfare.

You realized early on that you wouldn't eradicate this . . . this . . . *whatever it is* by yourself. There were too many of them. Their numbers increased faster than you could ever take them down. It would take thousands of hours and billions of bullets to destroy them all . . . and even then, it might never happen.

Your job is to learn. Learn to survive.

On your journeys through the creaking, hazardous city, you figured out what to take and what to leave behind. So-called survival gear, the kind sold at sporting goods stores and army surplus outfits, is almost always useless. Rambo knives and mosquito netting aren't much good against something that needs to have its brains taken out before it stops moving. Ditto for hunting rifles—unless you're going to be spending the apocalypse hunkered down in a clock tower, there's no need for a weapon that requires forty-five feet of aiming distance.

Everything you were taught about survival, you realize, was really just *hunting* information. How to cross a river, how to camp in the woods without freezing, how to stalk and drop a deer.

Only . . . *you're* the deer now. There are thousands—maybe millions—of hunters walking through the city, every moment of every day, and they can't be scared off. They don't get cold. They don't need to hunker down and sleep.

They never quit hunting.

Digging a *hole* seven feet deep and across would be hard enough; digging a seven-foot *trench* encircling the entire house . . . that would take months.

You nearly groan in exasperated frustration, but catch yourself. *No noise.*

You think of how you strengthened and secured your home's weak spots. The endless hours spent gathering food and ammunition. Your sister and mother . . . all that remains of your family. You clench your fists, then open them again, exhaling slowly.

No one's going to do this for me. Let's just . . . figure it out.

Your hand hesitates over a stack of books. After a long moment, you rummage until you find what you're seeking: a ninth-grade physics primer.

Two hours later, you think you have the answer—now for the second half of the plan.

We should get a few more shovels, says your brain.

You don't respond. You're busy flagging two pages on napalm.

You're not seriously making napalm, your brain asks, a trifle worried.

No, you reply, *but I do want to figure out how to burn those things once I catch them.*

Zombie Economics is about fighting the horde on its own terms—about coming face-to-face with the unthinking financial menace and giving as good as you get. It's also about maximizing your defense—about making sure that hand-to-hand combat is rarely, if ever, necessary.

Encircling your home with the trench—a basic yet constant layer of external security—makes for a better night's sleep and a more confident outlook. You know that a barrier exists between you and the undead . . . leaving you more time and energy to address other facets of survival.

In this chapter, you'll be shown five simple, powerful financial trenches . . . weapons that will stand guard, even when you can't. Like a physical trench, these five weapons are self-operating—once the initial setup is complete, they function on their own, with only basic maintenance required.

Remember: These weapons alone won't *save* you, but they will slow the advance of the zombie menace—they offer one more layer of security.

Trench #1: The Autopay

We touched on this in chapter 2; now it's worth taking a longer look. Setting as many of your recurring bills as possible to autopay works to your advantage in several ways. First, it helps guarantee that you no longer rack up late-payment penalties or exorbitant interest. Second, it works as an external inducement to cut unnecessary spending. With the knowledge that X dollars a month are already spoken for, and with the autopay ensuring that the money is coming out of your bank account no matter what, you have little choice but to make sure the money is there.

Think of it as the irresistible force meeting the immovable object—if your monthly autopays exceed the money in your account, you are faced with two choices: reduce your recurring expenses (there is always, always room to cut), or cut the amount you spend on non-essential items. If you don't face down your financial reality and make a decision, you will be penalized by late fees and, potentially, the loss of one or more of your services. Come home to an apartment with no lights or hot water, and you'll likely rethink the way you're dealing with your money.

Trench #2: The Vanishing Fifty

Similar to, but different from, the autopay, this weapon puts you on the other side of the trench, effectively shielding your savings (or a small part of it) from you entirely.

The way it works is simple: First, you have your bank set up an additional savings account in your name. Most banks will do this for little or no fee; some require a very small amount be deposited at the outset, but most will waive this requirement for an existing customer. Next, ask your bank to set up an autodeposit from your primary savings or checking account *into* this new savings account, in the amount of fifty dollars a month.*

What's next . . . is nothing. Don't ask for a credit card for this account. Or a debit card. Even an ATM-only card is to be avoided. Ensure that access to this money requires a physical visit to the bank.

By placing this money in a quasi-isolated account, you have killed

---

* If your situation is precarious enough that fifty dollars a month seems untenable, you may begin at twenty-five dollars a month, but no lower; the weapon doesn't work if there's insufficient ammo. What do you do with this collected pile of vanished fifties once it's reached a sizable amount? This is your indulgence money.

many zombies with one stone. To begin with, it's simply less likely that you'll break down and blow the savings on a pair of zebra-stripe seat covers if you're obligated to go to the bank, fill out a withdrawal slip, stand in line, and ask for the money every time you get the urge. Moreover, this vanishing fifty gives you the illusion of having a slightly smaller budget than you actually do. In reality, will you know the money exists in a separate account? Of course you will. But your brain is a tricky thing: when something is presented as fact, we tend to operate as though it is fact, even when we know better. This is why many people depend on the age-old tactic of setting their alarm ahead by twenty minutes: your conscious self may know the difference, but your primal self sees the information and reacts accordingly, keeping you from oversleeping . . . or overspending.

Trench #3: Paper, Not Plastic

Earlier in this book, we discussed the creeping menace of credit, and the damage it can cause to home, sanity, and future. This trench is a one-step method of keeping the credit zombie out of your home, off your street, and away from your neighborhood.

Don't carry a credit card. Ever.

Unless you are leaving the house to make a *specific* purchase, your credit cards need to stay buried at the bottom of a drawer. If they're not with you, they can't get loose and spread their sickness to the rest of your financial existence. For day-to-day purchases, keep a limited amount of cash on hand. (And when we say "limited," we mean exactly that—pick an amount and don't carry more than that amount at any one time.)*

---

* Incidentally, the excuse of carrying a credit card "for emergencies" is a fairly thin one. What actual, real "emergency" could a credit card possibly help you with? Tornadoes don't take plastic, and hospitals have no problem billing you. The only quasi-legitimate answer is "car trouble," but unless you're going on a cross-country excursion, the price of having a cab take you home (where the credit card resides) is minuscule compared with the money you'll save by not having it within arm's reach every day.

Online purchasing can be a danger zone for those with a credit card weakness.

To this, we respond with the cold, hard facts: extreme situations require extreme responses. If you treat the Internet like a store that never closes, it's time to get serious, even if it means being silly.

Freeze your credit cards inside a bowl of water. Sound ridiculous? You bet. Effective? You tell us. We have a sneaking suspicion that if you ever find yourself in the kitchen, chipping ice off your AmEx card so you can buy a bamboo steamer, you'll have what addicts call "a moment of clarity" long before you finish the job.

Eventually, you won't require such drastic measures; your spending and saving habits will be deeply ingrained, and those cards won't pose such a critical threat. In the meantime, keep them away from your wallet, your purse, your money, and your life.

Trench #4: Make Yourself Accountable to Someone Else

While Zombie Economics is about personal responsibility—about making the right decisions for yourself and your situation—there's nothing wrong with applying a little external motivation in the form of a friend or loved one. Their job? To keep you honest.

When you face a particularly challenging goal—such as limiting your credit card use or maintaining your job search despite numerous rejections—you may, over time, be tempted to downgrade your standards and expectations. Rules and limits you once considered sac-rosanct may gradually go by the wayside, victims of neglect and rationalization. Three job inquiries a week become two . . . or one. Your hard-and-fast prohibition against high-priced coffee drinks or convenience store lunches slowly becomes more of a "guideline" than a "goal," until, before long, it's returned to what it was at the outset: a bad financial habit you feel powerless to break.

If, on the other hand, there's someone who's privy to your plan from the outset—someone who knows exactly what you're trying to change or accomplish—and if that someone can be trusted to ask you point-blank about your success or failure in that regard, then those behaviors become far less easy to fudge. It's one thing to lie to your-self, but you'd be amazed how much more difficult such prevarica-tions become when they must be said, out loud, to another person. Moreover, if you're dealing with someone who knows you fairly well, they're likely to spot any such waffling the minute you attempt it.

Of course, this requires finding the correct person for the task; someone who's too lax in their queries will have no effect at all, while someone who treats every update as an interrogation will have en-tirely the *wrong* effect, as you'll likely begin avoiding these interactions altogether.

If at all possible, this role should be filled by someone who is, himself or herself, working through issues of financial or personal responsibility—or who has dealt with such things in the past. It's not necessary that the person be a flawless individual in this regard, only that he or she shares your commitment to addressing these potential weak spots.

Remember: This person's job (and yours for the person) is not to lecture or excuse, but simply to help keep the relevant issues in focus—to give an objective spot check, so that you can more easily track your progress.

You might feel that no one in your circle of acquaintances quite fits the bill in this regard. There are other approaches,* but know that all of these methods are an adjunct to your own self-assessment—operating with the knowledge that your progress must be checked and rechecked; that nothing can be taken for granted.

Trench #5: Tell Your Bank to Disallow Overdrafts

Presumably created to reimburse banks and lenders for the time and trouble of processing bounced checks, the overdraft fee ballooned into its own profitable side business with the introduction of the debit card. Consumers who failed to keep a close eye on their bank balance ran hundreds of dollars into the red, never knowing that every three-dollar soda was costing them an additional twenty-five dollars in overage penalties. Like a credit card charging 1,200 percent interest, the debit card became a loaded gun—one made even more dangerous by its complete and total silence.

Beginning in 2010, banks were forced to change the way they handled this process; consumers' accounts must now, by default, be set to disallow any purchase or transaction that exceeds the available balance. If you have fifteen dollars to your name and you attempt to make a sixteen-dollar purchase, the card will come up "declined." Potentially embarrassing—and far better than adding a twenty-five-dollar overdraft fee to that sixteen dollars. (And far, *far* better than ringing up a whole *day's* worth of shopping, only to realize that each and every purchase comes with its own overage penalty.)

---

* Online communities are one example, though it can be easy to lose hours of your life in such surroundings. If necessary, set limits on how much time you spend in these environments. For those who require a real-world component, most cities have at least one organization that meets to discuss financial responsibility and behavior. Though often similar to the recovery/12-step dynamic, these meetings are simply one more option for those wishing to have an outside perspective on fiscal choices and self-discipline.

Banks have responded by playing on their customers' fears, describing dire scenarios in which consumers are stranded or imperiled because of the inability to overdraw their savings account. As with credit card scare stories, however, the reality is far less frightening, primarily because true emergencies are few and far between, and those that *do* happen will not be mitigated by having a debit card.

Contact your bank—or whatever institution handles your checking/savings account(s)—and instruct them to *disallow* overdrafts on any and all accounts in your name. Do not be dissuaded by their protests; do not be convinced that you are putting yourself in jeopardy. You are doing quite the opposite: you are placing additional protection between yourself and the ravenous mouths of the undead.

TO REITERATE: The above five strategies will not, in and of themselves, save you. Make enough poor decisions, and no trench on Earth will forestall your demise. What these actions *will* do is augment and buttress the other strengths and weapons you possess.

The Trench buys you time.

The Trench gives you breathing room.

The Trench makes it easier to sleep.

This is what a rendering plant smells like, says your brain, if it were located inside a sewer.

You nod, and shovel a thick helping of ashes and grease out of the trench and onto your lawn. Clouds of flies appear almost instantly, then buzz away into nothingness; they won't go near the zombie sludge . . . nothing will.

Piles of dirt cover the lawn—you spent every free moment of the last three weeks digging the narrow ditch that circles your home.

"Narrow" is a relative word, however: the trench is two and a half feet across. This means that even a physically intact zombie—one not missing limbs or badly decomposed—will, when walking toward the house, stumble into the chasm; it's too wide to step across.

The depth, at two and a half feet, is just as crucial. Standing in the trench puts a zombie's knees below ground level, and simple physics traps them in that spot forever. They can't climb, and clambering out of the trench requires a surprisingly complex interplay of movements. Leaning forward and clawing at the ground isn't sufficient to overcome the problems presented by gravity and positioning.

Once the ghouls are immobilized, you assess the danger they pose and act accordingly. Some are dispatched with a crowbar (the shovel head is too valuable to risk). Their sickening movements end with a quick blow to the skull.

Others have fallen onto their backs, or are simply crippled or legless to begin with. These horrible specimens are often scrabbling at the trench's dirt floor, their jaws snapping open and closed with repetitive, mindless menace. Rather than risk the clutch of an undead hand, you simply pour a splash of gasoline onto the flailing creature, then light a small twist of newspaper and toss it into the pit. The writhing collection of rags and teeth goes up in flames, its claws and mouth clenching over and over, until it's . . .

. . . *until it's this,* says your brain, horrified by another shovelful of dripping zombie residue.

Every week or so, you bag the remnants into garbage sacks and haul them a few blocks away in a large gardener's wagon. Plenty of abandoned cars still have gas, but the roads are clotted with wrecked or zombie-filled autos; it would take hours to go even a mile or two, and if a swarm appeared, you'd be caught . . . and likely cornered.

In the first week alone, twelve creatures wound up in the trench. That was a disturbing dose of reality . . . especially because you often discovered them in the morning. That meant even without the lure of noise or lights . . . *while you slept* . . . there were zombies coming within a few feet of your house.

You were reminded of something a Florida lifeguard once told you: "If people knew what came within ten feet of them on a regular basis, they'd never go in the water again."

You check the trench. Clean. *For now.*

You climb out and carry the shovel toward the porch—it's time for some water and what passes for sleep. Then you hear the sound of an engine. A car. No . . . bigger than that . . . a truck.

What the . . . ?

Generators are the only engines heard with any kind of regularity these days, and even then, not very often. People keep them tuned up, but rarely running—no sense in announcing your presence . . . to anyone.

Before you can think further, a white panel truck rounds the corner at the end of the street. It's moving slowly, navigating the forest of debris, wreckage, and other automobiles . . . many of them burned-out shells. You stare silently, unsure of what to do.

The van slows to a halt in front of your house, its passenger-side tires up on the sidewalk. The driver waves.

Glad he did that, your brain says, *we might have missed him otherwise.*

Before you can react, the passenger door opens, and a man in fatigues leans out. "Let's go," he says. "We're getting everybody out of here."

"What?" you say . . . but you heard him perfectly. You're suddenly aware of how bizarre you must look: covered in dirt and sweat, clutching a shovel, the smell of gasoline and burned, rotten flesh filling the air.

The man laughs, giving a large grin as he steps out of the truck. He's wearing a camouflage cap and thick, black boots. He walks toward you and puts out an arm, his hand opened wide.

"C'mon, let's go. They've found a cure."

CHAPTER NINE

WITH FRIENDS LIKE THESE, WHO NEEDS ZOMBIES?

AVOIDING SCAMS, HUCKSTERS, AND OTHER FINANCIAL PREDATORS

They've found a cure.

His words echo through your ears, warping and distorting . . . like repeating your own name until it's gibberish.

You know you're supposed to say something, but there's just a buzzing emptiness; your brain seems to be on a coffee break.

Almost imperceptibly, your grip on the shovel relaxes; you slump by half an inch.

You turn and gesture at your house—God knows why. Your mouth opens, but all that comes out is an open-ended vowel sound: "I . . ."

You turn back to the tall, smiling man.

You imagine walking into a safe, secure building . . . some sort of gathering place for survivors. You can practically hear your mother's voice, relieved and exhausted.

God only knows what they've been through since leaving Dad . . . behind . . .

"I . . ." you say again, then shut your eyes long enough to focus your thoughts. You look at the truck, then back to the khaki-clad stranger. "Where are we going?"

"There's an inoculation center about three miles from here." The man cocks his head slightly. "Where have you been? We've been covering this area for days. Didn't you hear the announcements?"

He's lying, your brain says, back from time off.

You shake your head, wondering how you could have missed it. Where have you been? You've been right here . . . you've been . . .

You turn toward the house again. Door unlocked, supplies still inside. Trench still needing some work.

"This your place?" The man is looking past you now, his voice a mix of curiosity and admiration.

You smile despite yourself, seeing your home as this man sees it: a well-stocked, well-protected fortress . . . a place where you could outlast the unimaginable. A place where—

"C'mon . . . let's go," he says, clapping you on the shoulder and gesturing toward the truck. "We'll have to come back for your things."

Your legs are slightly unsteady, partially from the nonstop work of digging (and then emptying) the trench, and partially from the idea that this might be over, that you might be closer to finding what's left of your family.

Your brain is more strident: *This is not how rescues happen. This is not how things work.*

You think of calm and peace. Food that isn't from a can. Windows that aren't blocked and boarded. Hot showers. An end to this grayscale nightmare.

Your brain continues its protests; you press the naggings down into a dark, smothering place.

You just want it to be true.

You walk to the truck's passenger door and step onto the running boards, preparing to pull yourself into the cabin. You nod at the driver, a slight man with a weathered face, and then pause, wondering how all three of you will fit inside this small space.

Your brain working to make itself heard, muffled but implacable.

"Oh, it's bigger than it looks," says the voice behind you. "We'll have you sit in the back section. We've got a few more stops to make."

A small wire-mesh door separates the cabin from the truck's back storage area.

You pause, half in, half out of the truck. "Who are you with?" you ask, looking from the driver to the man outside.

"We're with the Fifty-first," he says, gesturing. "Get in the back . . . we'll tell you the rest on the way."

Get out. Get out now. your brain shouts, free of its restraints.

Time seems to stretch, the next few moments unfolding in what feels like slow motion. You see the driver's tangled hair, the faded, ripped stickers on the truck's dashboard—impossible to read, but haphazard, like a kid stuck them on . . .

Your eyes look straight through the steel screen door into the truck's back section.

There is no cure.

And they're going to kill you.

We've been programmed to believe that people are fundamentally decent, that when the chips are down, we stick together, bonded against a common threat. And it's true, for the most part.

But only for the most part. The full picture is far more complicated, and not nearly so flattering.

Crisis draws predators. Like vultures to carrion, they appear in the blink of an eye, their motivation simple: to take from others. While the more upstanding among us work to protect their families, loved ones, and even strangers, less-principled humans turn against their own, using chaos and confusion as opportunities to steal and betray.

Though a constant, inescapable part of life, hucksters and thieves are especially dangerous in a Zombie Economy—shifting and morphing from one situation to the next, victimizing those who are most vulnerable. Some look exactly like the swindlers they are, while others come equipped with a smile, a handshake, and feigned concern for your well-being. Some use scams as old as the hills; some hide their manipulations in fine print and minutiae. They are all—*all*—greedy, amoral thugs, using your fear and uncertainty against you.

Thankfully, these loathsome traitors, like the undead themselves, can be identified and their risk minimized . . . though never eliminated.

In this chapter, you will learn many of the tactics used by financial manipulators, as well as the language used to cloak their deceit. Though far from comprehensive, this information will assist you in discerning truth from falsehood.

These can be your first clues that something shady is afoot. And, when in doubt, *trust your instinct*—it's the most finely tuned risk-detector there is.

While many of the warnings in this chapter might *seem* obvious, remember: Every decade has seen a clutch of shrewd investors bilked out of their fortunes . . . often by a well-credentialed hustler who talked a good game and lured them into the con with an impressive résumé and references.

Common Tactics

Just as all the undead share certain behaviors, so, too, do most financial manipulators. Learn these methods of attack; doing so will make you far less vulnerable to them.

Limited-Time Offer/Act Now!—The oldest trick in the book, it pressures you to make a decision before you have the time to think it through. Suddenly, you're in the checkout aisle, clutching a bag of fifteen fluorescent T-shirts, wondering what the hell happened. *Only* respond to a limited-time offer if the item is something you *truly* need and would have purchased anyway.

As always, you must be truthful with yourself. Do not work backward from the assumption that you *will* make a purchase, looking for a justification. Begin with the most important question: "Do I need this?" and arrive at your answer honestly.

Final Sale/Closeout—Usually accomplished with large, gaudy signs that scream GOING OUT OF BUSINESS, this approach masks the reality: savings inside the store are likely minimal. A good rule of thumb is to make a "clearance" purchase only if the product is something you already planned to buy and is *at least 30 percent lower than standard retail price*. Anything less, and you're not dealing with a true closeout sale.

Don't Pay for a Year—A scam tailor-made for people in financial crisis. In truth, you are not just postponing payment, you are likely *adding* to it. The one-year period is treated as a *loan* from the business to you, and at the end of the year, payments begin—frequently at a sky-high interest rate. The bottom line: You'll spend more—often much more—than if you had paid in full with cash. Read the fine print.

Interest-Free for 36 Months—This is an innovative variation on the "don't pay for a year" scheme. In essence, a company agrees not to charge interest on your purchase payments for thirty-six months. However, the minimum payment on your new television (or whatever) is too low to allow you to pay off the full amount within the interest-free period. When the thirty-six months are up, your interest rates will jump dramatically—sometimes as much as 29 percent. And, as a horrible bonus, you'll still have a sizable chunk of the item to pay for.

Get a Store Credit Card and Save—Every major retailer has a variation on this scheme. ("Sign up for our credit card and save 20%," etc.) These cards are dangerous because many stores charge an annual fee for their card, and you may pay out everything you save. Additionally, the cards often have incredibly high interest rates.

The *only* time to accept one of these offers is:
- If there is no annual fee for the card.
- If you have only one or two other credit cards.*
- If you are doing this to save serious money on an essential item that you (say it with us now) would be purchasing anyway.
- And most important, if you can pay off the charge in the next month.**

Lexicon of the Living Dead: Words to Watch Out For

The undead are, for good or bad, horribly distinct in their appearance. Their rot and disfigurement, while sickening and terror-inducing, does have at least one benefit: they're easy to identify. Similarly, financial deceivers have their own specific traits. Watch out for the following terms and expressions—they appear in job offers, financial transactions, and marketing/advertising materials, and are often the giveaway that you are dealing with a financial predator:

"Commissions"—While there *are* reputable jobs that operate on a commission basis (primarily sales positions), the term is also frequently used as a lure in home-based business schemes. Typically, such rackets require you to pay significant "fees" for the right to earn commissions. Those fees may be the only real money changing hands.

---

* Fun Fact: Having numerous credit cards can hurt your credit score.

** If you do this, do not cancel the card immediately—that, too, can affect your credit score. Instead, keep a zero balance on it for two years and then consider canceling.

"Distributor"—This term is often (though not always) a tip-off to a **Pyramid Scheme.**[†] If a company wants you to sell or distribute their product, make sure they will buy back all or most of any unsold inventory. Also: make sure they focus more on the product itself than on the need to recruit other sellers/suckers. Yes, every pyramid scheme has someone at the top—someone who might (or might not) be turning a profit. But even if that were true, do you *really* want to stake your financial future on selling hand lotion to your aunt Bertha and her bridge club?

"Everything Must Go"—Often, this is the bait to a mediocre or worthless sale, especially if it's merely the closing of a specific branch/location. They may *say* "everything must go," but companies often shift their unwanted inventory to other branches or sell it in bulk markets. Translation: they have a use for everything, and it doesn't involve giving you a huge discount.

"https"—Any secure Internet site (especially one where money or credit card numbers are used) should have an address beginning with "https" (instead of the usual "http"). Some defrauders, however, are experts at faking a site's legitimacy—including the use of an "https" prefix. Always check a site's *full* URL—it may look like your bank, but it might be a fake. When in doubt, verify online transactions via phone.

"No Risk"—This is a lie. Every time. Act accordingly.

[†] **Pyramid Scheme** (*noun*): A moneymaking strategy—usually of dubious benefit—based on a participant's ability to recruit other participants into the arrangement. Will frequently lead to embarrassing, late-night discussions in which a participant attempts to sell boxes of detergent to annoyed loved ones.

"U.S. Treasury Direct Accounts"—A phrase used in numerous frauds, especially those conducted via e-mail. The term is meaningless in real life.

Beware the "Join the Elitists" pitch (Part 1). Whenever you are offered a stay-at-home business opportunity, a "fantastic revenue-generating system," or anything else that implies a life of indulgence (while requiring little actual work), you are probably being hustled.

Beware the "Join the Elitists" pitch (Part 2). Look closely: Is the offer being made by someone standing on the beach? Holding a tiki glass? Flanked by several improbably proportioned models and a Ferrari? You are *definitely* being hustled.

The elite do exist, but they won't offer access to the good life using an infomercial.

The Lowest of the Low

During the zombie apocalypse, there walk among us creatures of such decayed, minuscule moral character that to call them human seems an overstatement. They exploit the vulnerability of those in true peril, feeding on their fears and desperation, and devouring their futures as wholly as any zombie.

These contemptible scavengers are most often found in the following areas:

Foreclosure—If you are facing the possible loss of your home, be *extremely* leery of any business or organization that offers to assist you. Schemes that take advantage of property/mortgage anxiety are too numerous to list.

Shady financial schemes adapt to changing conditions, and are most prevalent during times of economic extremes—when things are either booming or busting:

When real estate markets are up, you are told to spend thousands to learn the secrets of buying houses cheaply—houses that you will, in turn, sell to others for profits beyond comprehension.

When real estate markets go south, you are told to buy "secret" foreclosure lists (or services that provide these lists) with the same end result: pennies for houses and resales to others.

Both scenarios are, of course, equally suspicious, and unlikely ever to generate a single dollar in profit. They are two variations on the same deceptive theme, each tailored to match a specific financial environment.

Debt consolidation—Often, this is merely a euphemism for bankruptcy: a middleman charges an exorbitant fee to arrange the same bottom-line "solution" that you could have initiated yourself (and at a lower cost). In the end, your credit and financial status may be even more tarnished than before. The "debt consolidation company," meanwhile, has pocketed your money and moved on.

The offering/"awarding" of nonexistent grants—Typically targeted at those who lack the financing for college or the ability to secure a business loan. The victim is asked to pay a "processing fee" or other such upfront payment. Ultimately, no grant money ever appears . . . because there *is* no grant. Keep in mind: *legitimate* grants must be applied for, and an extensive amount of paperwork is required. They are not easily obtained, and anyone who tells you differently is angling for a con.

Credit-score restoration—Companies that offer the means to "fix/repair" your credit rating should always, always, always be distrusted. The short, simple rule to remember is this: *No one can remove or alter credit information if that information is accurate.*

 RED FLAGS: LEGITIMATE INSTRUMENTS THAT CAN BE USED FOR ILL

CASHIER'S CHECKS: Incredibly easy to counterfeit. Do not accept these as payment.

MONEY ORDERS: Similar to cashier's checks, these also can be counterfeited, so avoid taking them as payment; money orders should also raise suspicion if someone is asking *you* to pay with one. *Never* hand over a money order until you have received all of the goods or services you expect. These are a principal instrument in scams the world over, because once a money order leaves your possession, your cash is gone.

SOCIAL SECURITY NUMBER: Never give out to anyone who *initiates* communications with you.

When in doubt, use the Internet to research a business offer or investment opportunity before spending a single dollar. While the net has its share of faulty information, there are numerous reputable websites dedicated to tracking and explaining common financial rackets:

- The Better Business Bureau (always a good place to start): http://www.bbb.org/
- The FBI's Fraud Database contains a constantly updated list of common scams and how to avoid them: http://www.fbi.gov/majcases/fraud/fraudschemes.htm
- For identity theft prevention tips, or to report a case of identity theft, contact the Federal Trade Commission: http://www.ftc.gov/bcp/edu/microsites/idtheft//
- ZombieEconomics.com. As an adjunct to the above, make certain that your computer has sufficient antivirus software installed. There are many free/low-cost options for this. Go to ZombieEconomics.com for more information.

Zombie Economics means full awareness of your surroundings. It means trusting your gut instincts and investigating further (or walking away) when something doesn't feel quite right. And it means protecting yourself against financial predators—including those that wear a human face.

They're going to kill me, you think.

You're half standing inside the cab of the truck, looking through the thick wire screen behind the seats into the vehicle's back storage area.

Tangles of blankets and clothing. Flashlights. Bottles. Food—in cans, bags, plastic tubs, and boxes. In a far corner, a small children's backpack is stuffed with packages of cookies. The outside of the backpack is covered with hearts and stars and bright red blood.

Near the backpack sits a large, open duffel bag—filled with Mace, pepper spray, and electric stun guns. Useless weapons.

Useless against zombies, your brain says, *not people.*

Before you can even process your thoughts, your body reacts, half falling, half leaping out of the truck and back toward the ground, a clumsy, graceless plummet.

Colliding with the man outside, you take a knee to the stomach. You crumple.

You're fading, things going soft and unfocused . . .

. . . something cold and hard strikes the side of your head. The pistol, gone from your belt.

. . . *why isn't he shooting?* . . .

. . . *too close,* the echoing answer of your brain.

Knowing you need to do *something*—another strike from that pistol and you'll never wake up—you wrap your arms around his legs and cinch tight. His knees bend outward, buckling. You twist your body; he loses balance, and you let yourself collapse, still holding his legs. He swings the pistol, but the motion contributes to his fall, and he drops, landing on top of you.

190

Now you're on the ground . . . grasping, struggling. You hear what sounds like mechanical coughing. You wonder if your lungs have been punctured.

Stay close, your brain yells, like a disembodied cornerman, *don't let him get enough room to fire.*

You wonder where his accomplice is. Any moment, you expect him to join the fray, firing his own gun, or kicking you in the back of the head.

Keep fighting, your brain says, focused on the now.

As you claw and tear, each of you fighting to get free or to stay close, you feel a dull snap; something has broken with a dry, splintering noise . . . something *major* from the sound of it, but it doesn't hurt. You can feel it jabbing into your body—

Into your body?

The shovel.

You twist onto your stomach. Your hands grasp the shovel and you do a sudden push-up, rolling both of you onto your backs. You instantly bring the broken shovel handle down like an oar into the water—you feel it connect with the man's soft midsection.

You don't wait—you get up on unsteady legs, and you swing the handle into his face, the jagged end leaving a diagonal slash. You still hear what sounds like a siren coupled with loud, mechanical clanks and grinds. You wonder if this is what life's last moments *really* feel like: no slideshow, just animal terror, loud shrieking, and a total circuit overload.

Where's the gun?

You catch a glint of something a few feet away—he must have lost it during the fight.

And where the hell is the driver? You can't understand why he's not wading into the fight. *He'll mace us both, load his pal back into the cab, maybe shoot me for good measure—*

Your brain figures it out: *They have guns but no ammunition.*

They're here to steal your ammo—probably after beating you senseless to see if you'll reveal any other hiding places.

That makes your next move a lot easier. You strike another blow into pseudo-military's face and dive toward that glint on the ground, hoping it's your gun.

Your legs are low on energy; you crawl the last few feet. That rasping, metallic cough is getting louder . . . maybe you're breathing your own blood. Your hands reach for—

Where's the gun? Where is it?

Look harder, your brain commands.

Your hands come up with a spray nozzle, meant for the garden hose.

For the love of . . .

You wait for the blow on the back of the head, the hissing of Mace, the heel of a boot. When nothing happens, you turn back, feeling for the shovel while you get to your feet.

The bloodied impostor is sitting on the ground, legs extended, not moving. Past him, you see the truck, doors closed, windows rolled up, engine running. Choking exhaust pours from the tailpipe.

The mechanical coughing . . . *the engine starting.*

The driver blares the horn . . . *the siren.* The noise barely registers as you walk toward the injured con artist, the shovel in your hands like a Louisville Slugger.

You hear the truck grind its gears and roll forward, the driver shouting something . . . his words a muffled thump behind the glass. *Probably leaving his friend behind,* you think. *So much for honor among thieves.*

You glance upward and stop, your feet paused in half-step, frozen.

The truck is vanishing into the biggest swarm of zombies you've ever seen.

You're stepping backward, off-kilter. *They're everywhere.*

To your left, a clutch of rotting horrors advances. You see a burst stomach, its contents trailing between the creature's legs.

You glance right; the truck is gone, enveloped by a sea of the dead.

Go, says your brain. *Go. Go!*

You take a momentary look at the still-unmoving charlatan . . . whoever he is.

Go . . . now, says your brain.

You turn. You run.

CHAPTER TEN

SETTING FIRE
TO THE HOUSE

WHEN YOU SHOULD
(AND SHOULDN'T)
DECLARE BANKRUPTCY

You know enough not to look back. Your feet hit the ground like a Teletype as you pound toward your front door, scanning the ground as you go: Shovel? Leave it. Pistol? It's back there, somewhere . . . gone.

You're on the porch . . . you're past the threshold . . . you're slamming the door shut . . . you're twisting the dead bolt and laying a crowbar across the frame, into the U-shaped hooks on either side.

Adrenaline pushes you through the house, from one window and door to the next, checking latches and locks and boards. In the kitchen, you bump into a glass jar of nails—it smashes against the concrete and linoleum floor. On the other side of the covered windows, the moans become almost a roar, increasing in pitch and frenzy.

You snatch a pistol from the kitchen table, check the ammo, and stand immobile. You hear nails and bones scraping against the outside walls. A slick of cold sweat covers your body.

You have no idea where they all *came* from, or even how many there are. You couldn't see past them, so there must be several dozen, at least. Your best guess is that the guys in the truck— whoever they were—drew the creatures. The two of them were probably rolling through town, maybe house to house, stealing, killing, whatever their unsavory motivations dictated. If they went slowly enough, made enough noise, they would have attracted at least a few zombies . . . then a few more . . . then a dozen . . .

And since they were stopping every hundred yards, the zombies kept closing in, kept getting nearer—like ghosts descending on a narcoleptic Pac-Man. They closed the final distance right as you were struggling with the khaki-clad impostor.

I guess we should thank those things for stopping the fight, your brain observes, *right before they tear out your windpipe, I mean.*

You don't reply; you're picturing the exterior of your house, wondering if you've missed anything. Did you leave a weak spot? A way in?

After ten minutes, the noise outside doesn't seem to be getting any quieter, but at least it's not getting louder. You don't hear any cracking or breaking sounds—the dam seems to be holding. You still need some kind of visual, though—you need to know what's out there.

You step gingerly across the kitchen floor and into the hallway; the chain for the attic hatch hangs down from the ceiling. You have visions of the panel swinging open and bushels of spiders pouring out. You don't know why.

You reach up and tug at the chain until the hatchway pops loose and the accordion-style staircase descends.

You climb up into the stuffy, cramped little room. At the far end, set a foot above the attic's wooden floor, is a large window that looks out over the front yard. You walk as silently as possible, hoping to get a glimpse of whatever's filling your lawn.

A loud, flat bang echoes through the air outside. Then more, in rapid succession. Gunshots. Nearby.

Your first thought is of the faux-military stranger . . . making one nonheroic last stand.

There's no way he's still alive, your brain responds. *He's inside some zombie's alimentary canal by now.*

Then who?

You slowly unlatch the window. There's no screen; it opens outward, like a door.

You strain to look without actually sticking your head out the window—those things can hear, and they can *see.*

Another volley of shots, coming from somewhere close.

You look down at the mass of zombies—easily a hundred of them, probably more. They're churning, bumping past one another . . . going toward the source of the noise. *They don't even know what it is,* you think, *they just attack anything that moves or makes a sound.*

That's when you hear the screaming: multiple voices mixed in with the chaos of gunfire and ravenous moans.

You were positive this block was deserted.

Forgetting yourself, you lean out the window. Two houses down, several people are standing on the roof, gathered around a ragged hole, pulling someone else out and onto the shingled housetop. One of the group—a balding, middle-aged man—screams and points down to the horde of zombies who, drawn by the noise and commotion, are slowly moving toward the house, drifting like one large, pulsing cancer cell. The others don't seem to hear him— then gunfire rattles the air; they're firing down into the hole . . . into the house.

Only part of the home's lower half is visible, but it's enough to tell the story: you see a squirming mass of ghouls shoving themselves through an empty door frame on the ground floor.

You wonder how many people have been hiding in that house . . . and for how long.

On the roof, a woman in a powder-blue vest is on her hands and knees. One of the others tries to give her a gun, but she won't take it.

Just stay still, you think. *Just stay still. If no one moves . . . if no one makes a sound, they'll stop advancing. They won't leave, but they won't attack. They'll just stay where they are—*

—until something else draws them away, your brain finishes.

Your mind races.

Think.

If you shout, make some noise, then the horde might come this way. Your house is fairly secure . . . it might withstand an assault while the others get away . . . maybe.

The people on the roof are hauling something else out of the hole. You look closer, squinting, trying to—

Oh, God, no . . .

It's gas. They've seen you setting fire to some of the zombies in the trench.

But there's no trench around their house . . . they'll—

You have to stop them, says your brain, the tone harsh and clipped, *stop them right now. Don't let them.*

"Hey!"

They turn to look. You're screaming, waving your arms, careful not to lose your balance. If you fall . . .

You shout again, waving a *no* with your hands. "Don't! Don't use that!"

They're looking, but saying nothing. You try again: "Just . . . just *don't move!* Just be quiet!" You realize how ludicrous this sounds. Now zombies are drifting back to your house in small groups. This division of their attention has also guaranteed that the ground *between* your houses is populated with zombies.

Goddammit.

They're not listening, your brain says, louder, *they're not listening.*

You watch the small group skittering from place to place, like roaches on a hot plate.

They can't wait, you realize. They can't even think.

You spin through plan fragments in your mind; could you

jump? Get out the front door and create some kind of distraction? Maybe . . .

On the housetop, a curly-haired woman has collapsed. She's staring blankly at you and sucking her thumb.

You look at the ground. At the roof. Your stomach fills with ice.

You scream, your throat going raw, *"NO! Stop!"*

They're pouring the gas.

I t is the scorched-earth approach to solving your debt. It is the sledge-hammer used when every flyswatter has failed. It is chemotherapy. It is nuclear.

It is burning down the house . . . on the off chance that it will save the occupants.

Derided by social critics, embraced too easily by flailing debtors, and a dirty word to almost everyone, bankruptcy is one of the most commonly referenced, but least understood, options in the financial arsenal.

We're going to walk you through this section a bit differently, utilizing a straight-ahead FAQ layout. This is for two reasons:

1. You are likely in one of two distinct camps at this point: strongly considering a bankruptcy claim . . . or having no such inklings at all. There exists very little middle ground.
2. Some of the facts regarding bankruptcy—its classifications and effects—are stark, black-and-white basics. The others are vast, sprawling thickets of legal obfuscation, navigation of which almost always requires professional legal counsel.*

In either event, there's only so much ink worth spilling on the subject, in these pages, at least.

---

* We're saying this now: If you are considering bankruptcy, you should speak with a lawyer. If you are filing bankruptcy, you must speak with a lawyer. If you proceed without a lawyer, you are throwing yourself into a zombie-filled cesspool. Fair enough? All right.

The *Zombie Economics* Bankruptcy FAQ

Q: *Should I declare bankruptcy?*
A: Wrong question. Try "What is bankruptcy?"

Q: *What is bankruptcy?*
A: Much better. Bankruptcy is when you declare, in court, that you cannot pay your bills, and you agree to steps taken *by the court* to erase or cut your debt. These can include:

- selling things you own
- setting up new payment plans
- forcing you to forfeit property for which you haven't fully paid

BANKRUPTCY SIX WAYS

There are six types of bankruptcy in the United States, each named for its particular chapter in the bankruptcy code:

Chapter 7—liquidation (sometimes called "straight bankruptcy"), the simplest form of bankruptcy

Chapter 9—municipal bankruptcy, for local governments

Chapter 11—reorganization, typically used by businesses

Chapter 12—for family farmers and fishermen

Chapter 13—for individuals with steady income who want to create a plan for payment of debts

Chapter 15—cross-border bankruptcy, used if you have property or debts in several countries

Most individuals file under Chapter 7 or Chapter 13. (More on the differences between the two later in this section.)

Q: *Why would I file for bankruptcy?*
A: Here's how the U.S. government puts it: "A fundamental goal of the federal bankruptcy laws enacted by Congress is to give debtors a financial 'fresh start' from burdensome debts."

Q: *A fresh start sounds fantastic. Where do I sign?*
A: Here's the thing: If you're seriously considering bankruptcy, it's a good bet that you've got substantial consumer debt, which, in turn, means you might not be so great at reading fine print. Let's be clear: Most people should think of bankruptcy as a *last resort*.

Yes, bankruptcy can clear away insurmountable debts you *currently* have, but it may also mean the loss of major assets. In a worst-case scenario, that can include your car or your house. And it will always, *always* put a large red mark on your credit report.

People should generally file for bankruptcy when it's their last/best/only way out of an inescapable debt trap.

Q: *So, should I declare bankruptcy?*
A: There is no one-size-fits-all answer (as you should have guessed by now), but we've put together a worksheet that will help you deter-

mine if you should *consider* bankruptcy. For now, we'll start with some basic questions:

Are you financially incapable of paying your monthly bills, with no realistic likelihood of that situation changing in the foreseeable future?

Are you facing lawsuits and/or collection agents and/or unable to pay money owed to the IRS?

Do you have zero savings?

Answering "yes" to any of these questions is an indication that bankruptcy may be appropriate. (For a more detailed questionnaire, go to the worksheet at the end of the chapter.)

Situations in which you may *feel* like you need to file for bankruptcy, but *shouldn't*:

- When it just seems like the easiest way to deal with a mountain of debt.
- If you find yourself saying (or thinking): "I don't care about the consequences, I'm just desperate to get out from under this debt."
- If you owe money to a creditor, but that creditor can't take anything from you for not paying. (This varies by state, but may include items such as a car or furniture.)

Q: *What are the pros and cons of bankruptcy? What would I gain/lose?*

A: Fantastic questions. Let's take a look:

PROS

- Bankruptcy can erase—or sharply cut—your debt.
- If you are earning a steady salary, you may be able to keep your house (and, possibly, your car).

CONS

- Bankruptcy can remain on your credit report for up to ten years.
- Bankruptcy will make it harder and more expensive to get new credit cards or loans.
- Bankruptcy can make it much more difficult to rent an apartment or buy a house.
- Employers are legally entitled to check your credit, and filing for bankruptcy could keep you from getting certain jobs.
- You may have to forfeit some possessions. (Of course, if you couldn't pay for them, you might have lost them anyway.)

Q: *My uncle Ted says that if I declare bankruptcy—*
A: What did we tell you about listening to your family? Your uncle might mean well, but he probably has *no idea what he's talking about.* There is a ton of bankruptcy misinformation floating around out there. Here's a sampling:

THE *ZOMBIE ECONOMICS* LIST OF BANKRUPTCY MYTHS

MYTH: Bankruptcy is too complicated.

FACT: It is not simple or short, but the bankruptcy *process* is relatively straightforward. (More info later in this chapter.)

MYTH: I can't declare bankruptcy if I have a job.

FACT: Not remotely true. Actually, you *must* have a job to file Chapter 13—the type of bankruptcy that allows you to keep your assets.

MYTH: Bankruptcy won't cover medical bills or credit card debt.

FACT: Bankruptcy covers most debt, including medical bills and credit cards.

MYTH: If I file for bankruptcy, I'll never get a credit card again.

FACT: You may not ever *want* one again, but after you declare bankruptcy, you can still get credit cards. The rates on those cards, however, will be significantly higher.

MYTH: I'll lose everything.

FACT: Not necessarily. Chapter 13 bankruptcy, in particular, is designed to help people keep major assets like homes and cars. Moreover, some states lay out specific circumstances in which such things are *exempt* from bankruptcy filing.

Q: *All right, I'm really, honestly thinking that bankruptcy might be a good idea for me. Which type of bankruptcy would apply to my situation?*

A: While you *may* qualify for other types of bankruptcy, the vast majority of individual bankruptcies are either Chapter 7 or Chapter 13. Here's a quick breakdown of each:

CHAPTER 7

TYPE OF BANKRUPTCY: Liquidation

OVERVIEW: In liquidation, the court appoints a "trustee" to assess all your assets and then liquidate them (turn them into cash), which, in turn, would go to your creditors. This could include your car, your home, and anything else you own.

RESULT: In Chapter 7 bankruptcy, the person filing is generally released from the debt they owe; it's erased, but they also lose most of what they own.

WHO IT'S FOR: Chapter 7 liquidation is for those who want to complete the bankruptcy process quickly. It is also for those who have no steady income.

BOTTOM LINE: Chapter 7 is simple and direct . . . like amputating your leg. You lose whatever debt is causing your financial disease, but you also lose any savings and any items of substantial worth.

CHAPTER 13

TYPE OF BANKRUPTCY: Repayment/Rehabilitation

OVERVIEW: In Chapter 13 bankruptcy, you propose a plan to rework your debt, usually lowering your monthly payments and/or the total amount you owe. Often, this happens through a bankruptcy attorney *you* hire; this attorney deals directly with the companies and people to whom you owe money.

RESULT: Under Chapter 13, you can set up a repayment plan allowing you to keep your home or car as well as other assets. This is why it's often preferable to Chapter 7.

WHO IT'S FOR: To qualify for Chapter 13 bankruptcy, you must prove you earn a steady income—the banks and judges want to know that you can consistently cover the new, lower payments created by the arrangement.

BOTTOM LINE: It takes longer to set up a Chapter 13 bankruptcy, and there are many more requirements, but it has major advantages.

Note: With both Chapter 7 and Chapter 13, you are making a legal, binding declaration of bankruptcy. As a result, some or all of your debt is erased and your credit record is changed.

Q: *So, if I decide to file bankruptcy, how do I begin? What happens first?*
A: One answer, in four parts:

1. Not quite yet. First, you should make one final attempt to *avoid* bankruptcy. We cannot stress this enough. Bankruptcy has a powerful, almost hypnotic pull for certain people. It seems (falsely) to be a simple, all-encompassing solution, one magical press of the financial do-over button. This is not the case. And even if it were, the potential ramifications are such that only fools would plunge into this "solution" without doing everything in their power to prevent it.

   Before you set things in motion, attempt a resettlement: call the companies and banks to which you owe money and tell them you would like to restructure your debt. Try to negotiate lower interest rates, lower monthly payments, and, possibly, even a lower amount of principal. State, in no uncertain terms, that you *want to pay back your debt,* but that your current interest rates and/or the overall amount make it impossible.

When negotiating for lower payments/interest/principal, remember that you are dealing with a business. When all is said and done, they want to get their money back, and *some* of it is preferable to *none* of it. You shouldn't act as though you're trying to strong-arm them—that will have exactly the wrong result—but be honest and up-front. Make it clear that you're *considering* bankruptcy, and that you would very much prefer to do the honorable thing— pay off the money you owe.

2. Get credit counseling. By law, anyone filing for bankruptcy must first *pay* to go through credit counseling.* This can be done over the phone or in person, and is handled by a credit-counseling business or organization that has been approved through the Justice Department's U.S. Trustee Program.** Officials estimate that the required counseling can be completed in one sixty- to ninety-minute session; the cost is typically in the area of $50, though prices do vary. Ask

---

* Yes, you heard us correctly: you must fork over some of your own cash before you can claim bankruptcy. If you cannot afford to pay for credit counseling (which seems likely), you can apply for a waiver.

** In Alabama and North Carolina, you go through court administrators called "Bankruptcy Administrators."

about the fee in your initial discussion with the agency; also ask for a detailed listing of what services they provide.

You must go through this credit counseling no more than six months (180 days) before the date on which you file your bankruptcy claim.

Hire a bankruptcy attorney. We can hear you saying, "I don't have enough money to *eat*. Now I have to hire a lawyer?" Trust us: you need a **Lawyer**.[†] There is no wiggle room on this.

Going through bankruptcy without an attorney is asking for trouble of the very worst kind. A lawyer will guide you through what is an enormously complicated process, and will, as part of the bargain, help to protect as much of your remaining cash and property as is allowable.

Search carefully: you don't need someone who will give you lavish treatment. You need an attorney who will handle your case professionally while charging the minimum amount possible.

As an addendum to "Always consult a lawyer and financial advisor," we'd like to offer a group of folks *not* to consult: everyone else. Other than your spouse/significant other or business partner(s), you should listen only to educated, licensed professionals when it comes to the bankruptcy option. Your friends, your family, your coworkers, talk-radio hosts, politicians, clergy, and the guy who cleans your rain gutters are all equally *unqualified* to take part in

---

† **Lawyer** (*noun*): (1) Person skilled in the understanding and practice of law, often a specific branch of law. (2) The only person who can protect you from another lawyer, or team of lawyers.

the discussion. They will confuse and contaminate what needs to be a clear-eyed, informed decision. Tell them after the fact, if at all.

3. Check out your state's bankruptcy law. Specifically, research while property and assets are exempt from bankruptcy in your state and under which circumstances. Yes, your lawyer should already be doing this for you, but it's to your benefit to familiarize yourself with how your state operates in terms of bankruptcy claims. This also makes it easier to assess the quality of work your lawyer is doing.

We'll give you one piece of legal information right now. If you owe alimony or child support, bankruptcy *will not* take those obligations away. You may be able to apply for reduced payments, but bankruptcy law makes child support and alimony continued requirements.

Bankruptcy is a legitimate tool, with real benefits . . . for those in dire enough straits to need it. If you're in anything less than critical condition, you will come out the other side even more damaged than when you entered. And make no mistake: even for those who qualify, bankruptcy is still a risk. When you burn down the house, there's every chance it will burn you back.

WORKSHEET #13: SHOULD I DECLARE BANKRUPTCY?

Things leading toward a "no" (check those that apply):

___You can pay all—or the vast majority—of your monthly bills.

___Your income will likely improve in the next three to nine months.

___You have *any* amount of savings in your name.

___You have *any* major assets (such as a car or house) in your name.

___You haven't asked your creditors about structuring a new payment plan.

___You could pay off the rest of your debt in three to five years if you drastically cut expenses.

Things leading toward a "yes" (check those that apply):

___You are being sued for missed payments and/or money you owe.

___You cannot pay your taxes.

___Your debts increase every month.

___Bill collectors are calling you.

___There is no way you could pay off your credit card, medical, or other debts within three to five years, even with a drastic reduction in expenses. (Do not include home or car loans.)

___As part of the above: You've gone through your budget and can't find *anywhere* to cut or any way to bring in significantly more money.

___You are at risk of foreclosure or of losing your car because of your other debts.

___Your mortgage, car, and/or credit card lenders have either (a) already lowered your payments, or (b) refused to change your payments.

Before you can think of anything that might stop them, several of the survivors two houses down have walked to the front edge of the roof, pouring a trail of gas on the undead horde below.

This is all wrong, you think, *they have no idea—*

But that's just it: they don't. Starving, filled with panic, desperate for anything that might end the standoff, they've reached for the biggest, bluntest, most uncontrollable weapon at their disposal . . . and they're using it. Anything you could say would be useless; they can't hear anything except their own shrieking fear . . . and a horrifying sound like ten thousand empty wind tunnels.

The gas lands on the zombies below, followed by a torch—some old rags tied around a chair leg.

The flames are immediate . . . and immediately out of control.

Cut off a zombie's arm, what happens? It keeps walking. Blind it, gut it, throw it down a dozen stairs, and what happens? It keeps walking. It keeps killing. It keeps walking and it keeps killing until there is nowhere else to walk and nothing left to kill.

Set a zombie on fire, and what does it do? It keeps walking. It keeps killing.

The creatures stagger forward, indifferent to the heat, indifferent to the burning crackle of their own bodies. Fire spreads from one . . . to the next . . . to the next. Without a trench to stop them, those walking toward the other house continue their march . . . and soon, the walls are ablaze.

Flames race upward. The house is doomed, though no one on the roof seems to know it. They're dashing from corner to corner, trying to burn the creatures into oblivion; the shimmering heat and thick, acrid smoke prevent them from grasping the true horror of their situation.

Watching the inferno rage, you doubt that they're even capable of comprehension at this point. You are seeing a collection of human minds spin through the last scattered, broken steps of their survival blueprint, skipping from one half-idea to the next, their thoughts as formless as those of the walking dead below.

Flames are inside the house now. Smoke pours upward through the hole in the roof. Zombies swarm into the house, filling it with sickness and claws and rotten skin on fire. Filling it with death.

The woman in the powder-blue vest is the first to jump. She makes it to the ground, landing on a soft patch of sloping grass. She runs toward the backyard, through a place where the horde seems thinnest. She falls. She gets up, now with a limp. They're closing in. She looks in every direction.

Nowhere to go.

She's torn to pieces while, on the roof, the bald man shouts at the three remaining survivors, his face red from panic and flames. He screams something, over and over. He begins to strip off his clothes. Two of the others—a tattooed man and a boy in his late teens—frantically take off their shirts, their belts, their socks. The curly-haired woman is sitting, unmoving, arms wrapped around herself. The others yell something to her. She doesn't respond. They turn away and begin tying their clothing into a long chain.

The fire is bending and warping the air. You see sections of the house sagging inward. The undead continue to push their way through windows and doors, their bodies and clothing set alight as they fill the home's interior.

Something moves in your peripheral vision; the prone body of the curly-haired woman is tumbling toward the edge of the roof.

The three men work with frantic hands, tying belts to shirts to jackets.

The woman goes over the side, down into a tearing, shredding sea of nails and teeth.

When you look back to the three men, only two remain; the teenager is gone.

The house is nearly engulfed. Only the roof's interior insulation has kept it from disintegrating already . . . now it begins to fall apart, one corner dropping into the fire below.

The two men are at the chimney; their hands scrabbling and clawing, their feet scraping . . . digging for a hold.

Below, the horde is growing and now stretches in all directions—seemingly for miles. Maybe there are no more humans. Maybe this is man's last stand . . . right here, right now.

The home's south wall collapses, and, with a sound like an old, rusty hinge, the roof follows, tearing away from the chimney and sending up torrents of sparks and burning debris. The ceiling crashes into the scattered ghouls below, obliterating some, pinning or trapping others.

The two men, screaming themselves raw, are clinging to the slender column of bricks and mortar, their arms straining, feet jammed against the stone with such force you can nearly feel it yourself.

Fifteen minutes later, after the home's last wall crumbles into cinders, the sound seems to flatten out, the blazing fire replaced by a rumbling crackle . . . and underneath that, the constant moan of the horde, like the endless, open roar of a waterfall.

The men straddling the chimney emit an ongoing stream of whimpers and hysterical gibberish.

You stand, immobile, unable to fully process what you have witnessed—you feel guilty, fascinated, horrified, fearful. You know that whatever your plans *might* have been, you're not leaving. Not now.

They would have filled the trench, you think, staring down at the narrow, winding trap around your home.

Those things would have walked right over their pals like a bridge, says your brain.

And I'd be dead, you think, remembering the sight of the ghouls, their rancid skin on fire, walking toward the screams on the other roof.

And you'd be dead, says your brain.

Through the smoke and the heat-warped air, you see them—the two men atop the chimney—slumped into each other:

Their bodies a series of small, shifting motions as they fight to keep their balance.

Their arms and legs twitching with fear and exhaustion.

Their sobs, dazed and uncontrollable, a high-pitched sound that carries with the wind.

Their every noise and movement keeping the zombies right where they are.

CHAPTER ELEVEN

NEVER GIVE UP, NEVER GIVE IN

HOLDING OUT FOR
AS LONG AS IT TAKES

Throughout the night and into the next day, you hear the mob of living dead grow in number and ferocity, drawn by the screams and wails of the two men atop the chimney.

You're guessing that in some alternate world—one where your life isn't being jeopardized—this is probably hysterical. You can see it now: jittery, jumpy, black-and-white footage of two schmucks inadvertently burning down their own house, ending up on a rickety pile of bricks, swaying back and forth . . . while down below, all the big, ugly, flesh-eating monsters decide to bother the guy next door. Hilarity ensues. Maybe the zombies will leave a flaming bag of intestines on your front porch and ring the doorbell, slowly shuffling away—

BZZZZZZZ.

You jolt back into reality, crouched by the front door. Your cell phone—useless now, except as an alarm—is vibrating in your side pocket. You click it off, looking at the time: you've been here for thirty minutes, waiting, listening. Wondering if a critical mass of ghouls would lean on the door frame, splintering it, or if one of them would catch fire in the still-smoldering wreckage outside, setting another home ablaze, then another, then yours.

Yeah, in some other world, this is probably hilarious. In this one, you've been awake for what seems like days, checking and rechecking the doors and windows. In this one, you're creeping from one section of the house to another, making sure that no noise comes from your footfalls as you inspect the boards, the nails, the draping.

With the trench nearly overflowing, you realize your survival depends on simple, specific things . . . like a few inches of plywood and cloth, and a bag of nails, and the fact that the growling, snapping horde can't actually *think.*

You have, in your darker moments, pondered killing the two men on the chimney. You've got ammunition, and a hunting rifle, and targets that are the very definition of "stationary."

On the other hand, you've also got hundreds—maybe thousands—of zombies outside your home, and getting their attention seems like a *bad* idea. If they start focusing on your house, they won't *need* to think—they'll just bump and scrape against the doors and walls until everything breaks and buckles and falls apart.

They can't know you're here.

So you sit. You move to another door. You listen. You sit. You move to another door.

You hope for the weak, almost childlike whimpers outside to just stop.

You wonder if you're in hell.

You work to keep your own sanity intact, shielded from the growing noise and chaos, from the nonstop dinner bell gibberish filling the wet, rank air. You think about where you'll go the next time you're able to leave the house. You pile books at every door and window; once you've checked for breaks and weak spots, you allow yourself a few minutes to read, momentarily escaping into another world. Any world but this one.

And you do what the people two houses down did not: you plan.

You've stockpiled ammunition. (*Enough to start your own dictatorship,* your brain says admiringly.) You've saved food, water, tools, first-aid supplies, and books. There's also a battery-powered radio and a case of batteries . . . though most of the dial is just static by now. The only station that comes in clearly has been looping the same fifteen minutes of news over and over again for months.

Now it's time to dig in. You intend to survive this siege, however long it lasts.

Working with equal parts speed and silence, you move as many of your supplies as possible into the attic . . . even the strongest door will break eventually.

Ammunition goes up first, followed by water, food, and tools. A pistol stays tucked into your belt; it goes everywhere you do.

You're kicking yourself over one huge omission: there's no opening in the attic ceiling. If you need to escape the house—if your food and water run out, or if, *heh heh,* someone decides to set a *roaring, irresponsible bonfire*—you'll have to *cut* a hole in the ceiling, and fast. You can't do it now; the noise would attract everything with mottled skin for five miles. But if you *need* to get out, it means they've broken through downstairs, and then it won't matter *how* much noise you make. You check the electric saws, their blades, and the generator: all intact, all working.

You bring up loads of books, pens and paper, a red police light, regular flashlights, a flare gun and boxes of flares. You don't stop until the job is finished—the attic now a fortress within a fortress.

You didn't start this nightmare, but you will outlast it.

The waiting is the hardest part.

Truer words have rarely been spoken. While waiting might lack the visceral thrill of, say, your house being repossessed, it's got a terrible series of attributes all its own. Like *worrying* about your house being repossessed. Like obsessing over your checkbook. Like scrimping, cutting, and saving. Like putting away your 10 percent and then figuring out how to feed yourself until payday.

The waiting sucks.

It's also an unavoidable part of Zombie Economics. Between "Making the Decision to Live" and "Victory" . . . is "Holding Out."

This chapter is about making it through; buckling down *for however long it takes.*

This will not be easy.

This will not be forever.

This is now.

THE FIRST THING to remember is the first thing you learned:

No One is Coming to Save You.

And even if they are, it may take months or years. You must take responsibility for your own survival, or your saviors will be rescuing a pile of bones.

There is no insta-fix, no overnight cure. There is only inch by inch, moment by moment. You cannot wish, hope, or pray your way out of this. Anyone who says different—all together now—is selling something . . . or has bought it themselves.

As part of the above, make sure you're not deluding *yourself.* Know that your survival is just that—you're *surviving.* You're holding out, and there's no telling when the danger will pass.

Be anxious. Be pissed off. Be impatient. As long as you're realistic. This will not be easy. This will not be quick.

TRACK YOUR HEAD SHOTS, TRACK YOUR SUCCESS

As you navigate the zombie landscape, things can easily become a blur. Ghouls appear . . . ghouls vanish in a haze of gunpowder and blackened brain matter. Over time, one day blends into the rest. You don't count, just aim and fire. Maybe you've killed fifty, maybe two hundred.

If you don't keep track of your time and your progress, you will lose perspective on your situation. In your personal economy, this will put you at a disadvantage when making further decisions. You will, for example, be much more likely to over- (or under-) estimate your savings and your debt level. You will also rob yourself of the vindication and power that come from seeing real, tangible proof of your advancement.

Numbers don't lie: your red ink, your living expenses, your credit score . . . these things all go up or down *based on your actions.* What could possibly be more inspiring than seeing the cold, hard proof that *you are making headway* through this nightmare?

On your weakest days, in your pessimistic moments, a daily/weekly/monthly log of your financial health can be invaluable—it is the reminder that you are winning, one inch at a time. It will reinforce your strongest choices and help to quash your dangerous leanings.

For tools on tracking your financial health, go to

ZombieEconomics.com. (To get online versions of the worksheets and advice in previous chapters, look for "Weapons" and "From the Book." The password is: Never Give Up Never Give In

Focus on Today, Live for Tomorrow

Zombie Economics means you fight. You fight and you claw and you don't ever give in. You shoot, you hammer, and, if necessary, you *punch* your way out. If you go down, you go down swinging, taking as many of the undead with you as possible.

Zombie Economics means living for tomorrow, not today.

"Living for today" is often a thinly veiled euphemism for "cowardice." Living for today means accepting the idea that you will never change, *can* never change. Living for today means just *accepting* whatever tomorrow hands you, be it a pink slip, a repo notice, or the news that your ice cream habit has given you diabetes.

You will focus on today . . . and live for tomorrow. This means never throwing in the towel, never giving up. It also means resisting the sometimes-powerful urge to *willfully make your situation worse.* And that temptation can be strong: The dieter who passes 250 pounds and gives in, hitting 350 the next year. The smoker who, ten years into the habit, says, "I gotta die sometime," and abandons the effort to quit. The spender who sees a mountain of debt . . . and feels the giddy urge to go all-out, maxing every credit card they've got, jacking their balance through the roof. The survivor who, cornered by the creatures, lies down and dies, only to be resurrected as a walking horror of themselves.

There is no majesty in doing the zombies' work for them, no glory in handing yourself over like a denim-clad canapé.

There will be setbacks and mistakes. You will stumble, and fall, and recover. But you will not give up. *You will live for tomorrow by focusing on today.*

WORSHEET #14: THE MAGIC NUMBER

A shotgun is worthless if you don't take aim. And every gun is meaningless without ammunition. To survive the zombie infestation, you need the undead in your crosshairs . . . and bullets in the chamber.

The Magic Number helps you do both . . . but only if you put it into action.

1. FIRST

Go to page 34 and find the amount in your Operating Fund. That's the money you have after paying bills and absolute necessities. (If you haven't calculated it recently, do so—you need to start with correct information.) Write that number directly below.

Monthly Operating Fund: _____

2. NEXT

Write down any purchases you need—or plan—to make before your next payday. These expenses could be anything—a gift, a business lunch, new brake pads, or anything else. Write those expenses here:

Expected Expense	Amount
_____	_____
_____	_____
_____	_____
_____	_____
_____	_____

_____   _____

_____   _____

Total those amounts:

TOTAL EXPECTED EXPENSES _____

3. NEXT

Subtract those expected purchases from the Operating Fund.

Operating Fund: _____

–

Expected Expenses: _____

=

MAGIC NUMBER _____

This is how much money you have to spend until your next payday.

THE END

Keep track of the Magic Number as you spend.

Enter the Magic Number above in the first space under "Magic Number Now." Write in the amount of your next expense and subtract to get your New Magic Number. Then move that New Magic Number into the "Magic Number Now" slot on the next line. Subtract your next expense. And so on.

Ideally, you should keep a rough estimate of your current Magic Number in mind at all times. This will tell you, cleanly and simply, how much money you have left until the next payday.

The point, incidentally, is to stay above zero . . . before payday, and always. Live your life, but pace yourself so you can *keep* living it.

MAGIC NUMBER NOW   -   New Expense   =   New Magic Number

_____ - _____ = _____

_____ - _____ = _____

MAGIC NUMBER NOW	-	New Expense	=	New Magic Number
_____	-	_____	=	_____
_____	-	_____	=	_____
_____	-	_____	=	_____
_____	-	_____	=	_____
_____	-	_____	=	_____
_____	-	_____	=	_____
_____	-	_____	=	_____
_____	-	_____	=	_____
_____	-	_____	=	_____
_____	-	_____	=	_____
_____	-	_____	=	_____

FINANCIAL STRENGTH

Financial strength is not about your income or your credit score. Financial strength is an attitude, a belief system—it is about how you behave today and tomorrow.

Financial strength is about the difference between savvy and reckless. It's about making choices—not just *knowing* what's right, but having the will to *do* what is right.

Help Is Not the Enemy

Walking the burned-out shells that used to be neighborhoods, you will, occasionally, cross paths with other survivors, many of them headed for specific destinations: a family member's home, a rumored safe house, the ocean. When possible, you share some of what you have: be it food, water, or a map. As your routes diverge, you wish them well, knowing that in a matter of days, their survival will once again be in their own hands. You realize that others might be less generous to strangers—but you realize something else: if the situations were reversed, you'd feel no shame in accepting help.

Self-reliance is key. Without it, you will live eternally on the combined mercies of luck and others' generosity. You must learn to stand for, and by, yourself. This does not, however, mean perishing within sight of assistance, or remaining mute as your food and resources dwindle and vanish. This does not mean rejecting help when you truly need it.

As long as you are honest with yourself and others, as long as you are honorable with your word and actions, there is no shame in accepting help . . . or asking for it.

If you lose your job, immediately assess your likelihood of finding another. If there is any delay in locating your next position, *file for unemployment.**

If you cannot afford to eat properly, apply for food stamps.**

If you have a family, and insufficient money to pay for their Absolute Necessities, there are additional forms of assistance available to you—use them. (For more information, go to ZombieEconomics.com; if you don't have Internet access at your home, the public library provides it without charge.)

None of these are permanent solutions, nor are they intended to be. Think of them as fellow survivors in the overrun city; their paths

---

* How? Go online and search for your state name and "unemployment," but make certain you look for the *state government–sponsored website,* not a private site that purports to advise you. Verify that your state allows you to apply online. (In the event that your state does not allow for online unemployment application, registering via phone is tedious and often irritating, but much faster than applying in person.)

** How? Food stamps (which stopped being stamps some time ago and are now issued as a debit-type card) are administered by the Supplemental Nutrition Assistance Program. Look online for that phrase and your state name (or "SNAP" and your state name). If you're looking this up in a phone book, search for "Department of Social Services" or "Department of Health Services."

intersecting with yours. If you need their help, ask for it. There is no disgrace in receiving assistance—there is only disgrace in giving up.

Other social agencies and nonprofit groups (both religious and secular) exist to help with specific issues: child care, housing, nutrition, etc. Some of these organizations work within a particular community or cultural group; others offer no-strings assistance to all who need it, asking only that you lend a hand in return, or that you consider a donation once your situation has stabilized.

DON'T BUY WHEN YOU CAN BORROW

Your friends have loads of movies they don't watch. Neighbors have big-time tools that they use only once a year. You have a library of How-to. Forget City Hall and the mayor. You need to help one another.
Do this with friends and neighbors:

- Put together lists of what you each own and would be willing to loan.
- Think about: tools, movies, computer games, board games, books, maps, camping gear, sports equipment, the javelin set you got as a graduation gift. You get it.
- Use free online tools to design and set up a community group or webpage. Include databases to show who owns which things and who has borrowed what.
- If possible, keep track of the raw lists through a spreadsheet. It will be easier to move and manipulate.
- Put together notes about businesses, from restaurants to florists, that you recommend or pan.
- Be judicious. Don't needlessly borrow or make any of this burdensome. It should be easy.

> • Enjoy. Potentially you'll be able to pick up a new movie
> or reciprocating saw in your bathrobe. For free. It's a
> beautiful thing.

When you're deep inside the zombie apocalypse, you cannot depend on being rescued by others—such naïveté will only leave you dead. The above options, though, *will* help to give you breathing room—granting you a few moments of reprieve so you can figure out your next move. If you act with **Financial Integrity**[†] —if you can look yourself in the eye and know you are doing your best—you are operating with financial strength.

[†] **Financial Integrity** (*noun*): (1) The consistent adherence to the fiscal rules and goals one has laid out for oneself after taking an honest inventory of one's financial life and aspirations. (2) The belief in, and practice of, honorable and honest interactions where money is concerned.

This attic isn't very spacious, says your brain, as you stretch out on the wood-plank floor.

I'll bring it up at the next homeowners' meeting, you respond, beginning your push-ups, *right after I complain about all the zombies on the lawn.*

And those guys on the chimney, your brain says, *isn't there a three-hours-of-screaming-per-day rule or something? We're never going to be able to sell this place.*

You stand and walk toward the attic window, careful to stay off to one side.

The horde is still there. The men are still screaming. You still have no solution.

So you sit. You think. You look out the window. When your phone buzzes every few hours, you eat, whether you're hungry or not. If you get sick or malnourished now, there's no way to go for help . . . no one to ask.

You make backup plans . . . and backups to the backup. *If they get in,* you think, sitting on the attic floor, sketches spread out in front of you, *if they even* start *to get in, I cut a hole and I go to the roof.*

The roof sucks, says your brain, *even the attic is better than that.*

If they get in, you respond, *they've broken through reinforced doors and walls. It's just a matter of time until the whole house becomes unstable. The attic floor could collapse.*

There's a pause.

Go to the roof, says your brain, *that works.*

Thanks.

And then?

You pause . . . leaning back against the wall, staring at nothing. Thinking.

Jumping is a possibility . . . though if you land wrong, you're toast; busted legs have side effects . . . like ending up in some monster's stomach. Even if you *don't* land wrong, the ground is swarming with zombies. Their moans carry, especially on calm, windless days. And the moans attract other zombies. And *those* zombies attract other zombies. On and on and on . . . maybe without end.

If I get on the roof, you think, *I'll at least be able to see in every direction. Maybe I can spot someplace to jump and land.* You look to the far end of the attic, where ammunition is sorted by weapon and stacked to the ceiling. Rarely has one habit paid such tangible dividends; even if you have to flee the house, you'll have enough firepower to give yourself a fighting chance.

I'll wait. I'll look. I'll plan. It's what's kept me alive this far.

All right then, your brain says, impressed.

You reach for a textbook. You scan the index, looking for anything that might help the situation outside.

Nothing.

You start reading anyway. You have to stay alert. You have to keep thinking.

You try to sleep. When that doesn't work, you pick up a deck of cards. You create math and number games to keep your thoughts focused, and to distract you from the—

You stop in mid-shuffle, listening intently.

Something's different.

You walk to the window. The swarming mass of zombies hasn't

gone anywhere. Your fingers nudge the glass; it opens on oiled hinges, just a few inches. Leaning forward, you try to listen *through* the creatures' moans. You hear one lone voice jabbering in the dim evening light. Slowly, you look outside. You can make out the form of one man atop the chimney, his limbs wrapped around the square brick tower. The other man is nowhere to be seen.

You feel a wave of gloom—suffocating, like your face wrapped in wet wool.

Your brain is quiet, sounding a million miles away. *You can't save everybody.*

I didn't save anybody.

Time passes. The sun disappears. Your alarm buzzes in your pocket. Dinner. You switch it off.

You know it's the truth . . . you *can't* save everyone. Especially people who—quite literally—threw gasoline on their problems.

You also know, with frustrated, helpless certainty, that *their* disastrous choices are something for which *you* are paying the price.

The windowsill vibrates under your hand. You barely have time to register the sensation before feeling the floorboards jitter beneath your feet. Your blood surges in an ice-cold rush.

The house. They're in the house.

In an instant, you're covered in sweat, but your hands are calm and still. You're already gathering up the backpacks you've preloaded for this moment. *I survived outside,* you think, *I survived in the house . . . I survived here in the attic . . .*

You look around, making sure you've got everything. *And now . . . the roof.*

And where then?

Time to find out.

And that's when you see a spotlight cutting through the darkness outside. It glares into your eyes, momentarily blinding you. Now it's aiming down, the bright circle of light jerking from spot to spot—onto the tree, onto the lawn, the trench around your house. It skips from place to place like a giant flea, illuminating the horde, now the tree again, the top of your garage. It's like some kind of automated security light, or—

It's a helicopter.

Adrenaline floods your system; your heart pounds like it's going to blow out of your chest.

It's a helicopter. It's here for—

You stare for a moment.

The guy on the chimney.

They don't even know I'm here.

In an instant, you're rifling through the backpacks, looking for the flare gun.

Got it.

You check the chamber: flare loaded and ready.

You look at the ceiling. You wish you had just *cut* that god-damned hole. *Just one more day—*

No time, no time, you cut yourself off, *they'll be gone soon.* Sooner or later, they'll figure out the guy on the chimney is out of his mind, and might be unsavable in any event.

You look out the window; the ground is covered with ghouls—maggot-filled mouths and filthy, slippery skin as far as you can see. *No way out,* you think.

The chopper is aiming its light down into the sea of monsters, training out farther and farther, assessing the number of hungry, moaning mouths.

You can almost imagine what they're thinking in the helicopter: *one guy . . . on a chimney, for Christ's sake. Probably half dead, probably insane by now. No way we'll get him up without hitting a tree or a power line, and too many of those things for us to land. Even if we get close enough, he's basically a skeleton at this point . . . he can't lift himself up, and if we try to hook him, we'll knock him down into the swarm. Let's make a note on the map that he's here, and if we can come by tomorrow or the day after . . . and if he's still alive . . . and those zombies have dispersed a little . . . .*

You hear the propellers increasing in speed, the engines whining higher.

The spotlight flicks off. It's pitch-black.

No no no no no.

Without thinking, you knock the window open with your right hand. You miss the frame and your knuckles break through the glass. You don't even feel it.

You look to where you last saw the helicopter. Careful to aim away from the oak tree that partially blocks your view, you aim the flare gun into the sky, and fire.

CHAPTER TWELVE

THE FAMOUS
FINAL SCENE

The flare gun kicks in your hand; there's a loud, flat *bang*. A thin trail of smoke zags upward from the attic window.

The reaction is immediate and terrifying—the horde screaming with one fractured, windy voice. It's like you've opened an airplane door at thirty thousand feet.

Their howls are accompanied by a slow, collective turn, their rotting, decrepit bodies twisting toward the source of the bright yellow light.

The flare is arcing, sputtering for a moment, now splitting into four. Each of the smaller bursts burns like a miniature sun, then trails off into nothingness.

You're already reloading the flare gun.

There's no guarantee they even saw that, you think. *They could be headed back home right now.*

Home.

You don't let yourself get sidetracked: every single zombie is converging on your house . . . the flares were impossible to miss, even if you no longer had eyes.

There's no way they don't get in the house now, you think, stepping to the window again.

You aim to the left of the oak tree and fire a second time. If the pilots saw the flare—if they saw *something*—you want them to see it again. If they didn't . . . if they're going somewhere else . . .

As you watch the flare glow, fragment, and disappear from sight, you wonder how long the flare stays active. It's entirely possible that you're inadvertently setting more fires with every shot.

Oh, I imagine we'll find out soon enough, says your brain, as you reload the chamber.

You decide to angle your shots higher, though—you'll reduce the odds of hitting that tree.

You hook a hand inside the window frame, then sit, straddling the sill like a seesaw—one leg inside the attic, one leg out the window. This distributes your mass enough—you hope—that it would take a profound act of clumsiness to fall. You aim the flare gun straight up . . . and pull the trigger.

Ten seconds later, as you watch the flare disappear, you realize you're basically hurling candles into the air with a rocket launcher—it's amazing they last at all.

This is why fire is a bad idea, your brain says as you reload. *This is why we have microwaves, and central heating, and electric lights—*

You interrupt this thought to look across the room. There, next to the radio and a spare box of tools, sits the red police light.

It's a flasher; once turned on, the reflector inside spins around—the classic "put this on top and go catch a bad guy" light. But it's not going on the roof of a car this time.

Even as you're kneeling, stringing bungee cords together—hands fueled by the fear that the copter won't be coming back—you're shaking your head at the plan.

This is crazy, you think; your brain's only response is an excited chuckle.

You wrap two of the hooked, elastic cords around the light and pull them snug. You thread a thin nylon rope through the jumble and tie the fastest, strongest knot you can.

You stand, and let the light dangle at the end of the rope. You jerk the rope a few times, watching the light bounce in its bungee cradle.

No more time.

You pause, stomach clenched like steel cables, then switch on the police light. Without a siren, the red dome's flashing, nearly silent operation seems ghostly.

You walk to the window and hook your left hand inside the frame. You test the windowsill with your right foot, listening for cracks or splits.

Nothing.

Your hands are slick with sweat. Your right hand stings, feels sticky and crackly. You look closer: you're bleeding from somewhere deep, between your knuckles. You see the broken glass where, earlier, you banged the window open.

Too late now, you seem to be saying more and more often.

You inhale and step up onto the sill, your left hand clutching the inside of the frame; the wood bows and creaks under your feet.

Beneath you, the swarm is moving like earthworms in a bucket. *They always say not to look down,* you think.

Like a man hanging off a trolley, you lean out as far as your center of gravity will let you.

The rope clutched in your right hand, the light hangs like a blinking pendulum. Flashing and turning. Flashing and turning. Drawing them like catnip.

That's not the only thing they like, says your brain. Blood from your injured hand trickles down the rope, dripping onto the monsters below. You see a blackened, partial tongue licking at the air. You look away.

You begin swinging the light back and forth, gathering momentum.

You realize, with grim amusement, that you can't remember what *kind* of roof you have. Flat? A-frame? Multileveled? Where the hell is the light even going to land?

Somewhere they can see it, your brain answers. The voice is determined, and full of unspoken truth: if this doesn't work, things will get a whole lot worse. The blinking light will draw them from everywhere. They'll never stop coming; they'll be miles deep by morning.

You think about the pistol tucked into your belt. *If I fall . . .*

The thought trails off, unnecessary. You wouldn't manage a single shot before being torn into bloody, shrieking pieces.

As you swing the light, blood from your hand spatters the side of the house, the ground, the upturned faces below.

The moans are cresting and falling like waves now; with each pass of the light over their heads, the creatures' growls grow more agitated and ragged.

Zombie-nip, says your brain, but you're not listening. You're swinging the light up and back, as hard as you can, and as the light arcs up toward its apex, you let go.

Something immediately feels wrong. You realize that you've miscalculated; the bungee cords around the light kept stretching—like swinging something from a Slinky.

The light angles outward, crashing directly into the oak tree you've been avoiding all night. The rope snarls around a branch; the light plummets, finally coming to dangle just above the horde. Close enough to see . . . not close enough to touch.

Fog rolls through your brain, the exhaustion and fatigue and anger and disappointment conspiring to throw a mental circuit breaker. You're dizzy for an endless second . . . then your legs give way and you fall back into the attic, one foot still on the windowsill as the rest of you hits the floor. Your brain goes dark like a flicked-out lamp.

After what seems like hours of churning, sleepless unconsciousness, you jolt awake, feeling as though you've been punched from inside your rib cage.

You see a recurring red flash on the wall, and it takes you a moment to recall the events leading up to your blackout.

The light.

The tree.

The light landing in the tree.

You groan. Not on the roof, where it would have been visible to a helicopter . . . while remaining unseen by the *billion zombies on the lawn*. No, it had to land *in the tree . . . right above them*.

You wonder how many zombies the blinking red light has drawn since you passed out.

Maybe they won't see it flash during the day, you think, and then, *If I'm absolutely quiet—*

If you're absolutely quiet while cutting a hole in the roof, your brain finishes, drily.

You realize you're back to your previous plan: stay higher than they can grasp, stay focused, stay alive. You start to wonder what— if anything—has happened to the remaining man on the chimney, but you find yourself staring at the attic wall. The red flash from outside is still visible, but the pattern is different . . . or the bulb is burning out . . . or it's growing dimmer.

Or the wall is getting brighter.

You wrench your whole body up, facing the window.

The helicopter is a few hundred yards away and moving in your direction, its searchlight scanning the ground, the house, the light hanging in the tree.

You're taking no chances. Making sure the helicopter is a safe distance away, you grab the flare gun, extend your right arm out the window, and fire upward. It's the most beautiful sight you've ever seen . . . or imagined.

You're on your feet, waving your arms in a scissoring-V motion and wondering whether you should set off another flare . . . when you see that the helicopter is dangling a mesh harness from its underside.

They see you.

You look at the attic ceiling. No opening; nothing but solid panels of wood.

I told you we should have paid extra for a skylight, says your brain.

"Next time," you say. For now, the attic window will do fine.

Hovering two hundred feet above you, the helicopter lowers the harness until it's outside your attic window. You reach out, leaning as far as you dare, but your fingers barely graze the netting. Looking up, you see why: your roof has a long overhang, jutting out several feet past the house at some points, and keeping the harness just out of reach.

You turn away from the window and scan the inside of the attic, looking for something, anything. . . .

Bungee cord, your brain says, and your eyes lock on one of the remaining hook-ended coils. You snatch it from the ground and you're back at the window; you're not giving them time to reconsider.

Using the cord as a kind of grappling hook, you latch on to the mesh webbing and pull the harness close enough to grab. It looks like a combination rope ladder and bucket, and it's heavy; like holding a pendulum aloft. If you're not careful, the damn thing will swing back out the window—taking you with it—before you've fastened a single strap.

Instead, you pull the entire harness into the attic, dragging it through the open window until it's splayed out on the floorboards like a spilled fabric store.

Conscious of the ticking time, you lift part of the jumbled harness and realize it's basically a bag made out of crisscrossing ropes, like an industrial-strength fishing net. This isn't supposed to hold a person at all, just boxes and cartons and—

Can we go? your brain interrupts. *I don't mind being a flounder if it gets us out of here.*

"Fair enough," you say, and you step into the middle of the collapsed rope tangle, all of it leading to a thick tether that trails out the window and downward, before snaking back up toward the helicopter.

Feeling absurdly like you're putting on a dress of some kind, you crouch, grab fistfuls of the netting in each hand, then stand, pulling the rope webbing up around you . . . ensuring that you're safely in the middle. Your feet stick out of the bottom, as though you were being hauled out of the water by a unlucky trawler.

Your arms holding the rest of the harness off the floor, you move to the window and lean down to grab the tether line; one or two quick pulls and they'll know to start reeling you up.

You feel the movement before your hands even close. The tether is sliding through your fingers like a cloth snake, slithering out the window and up into the night sky.

Oh God—

They're pulling us up NOW, your brain says, in the closest thing you've heard to panic.

Your thoughts riffle through a thousand different plans, steps, safeguards—flashing past like calendar pages in a black-and-white film.

Get ready to jump, says your brain.

"What?"

JUMP. . . we have to JUMP, your brain says, no longer quarreling, but ordering.

You see more of the excess tether line—hauled in with the harness itself—sliding over the windowsill and upward, as though it were fixed to some heaven-bound conveyor belt. Up, up, past the roof, past the . . .

Then you understand. Up above, at the top of the house, the roof overhang is pushing the tether line out past the rest of the house by a few feet. As soon as the line reels up enough to pull you from the attic window, you'll swing out—

—*just like a pendulum,* finishes your brain.

And smash into that goddamned tree.

You grind your teeth, already wondering what it will feel like to be dragged into the open air and then right into a snarl of branches. And how long after that before they decide to cut their losses and *leave* you stranded in that hideous tree, directly across from your attic window, but unable to get back in—or down, for that matter.

The ground is covered with zombies, you think, cringing.

We've already done the whole "stuck in a tree" thing, your brain says, pointedly. *No point in revisiting the past.*

I am *not* staying here, you think, looking out the attic window. On the lawn, the zombies—maybe *all* of them, it occurs to you, from *everywhere*—swarm like maggots on a dead animal.

No way, no how.

Looking out the attic window, you see the oak tree, a mass of jagged branches and tangles, any one of them primed to snarl your harness . . . forever.

Below that, though . . .

You see the wide, heavy lower portion of the tree: rough, covered with sharp, unforgiving bark, but free of anything that could realistically catch or clutch you.

Except for the zombies, of course, your brain says.

"Well, sure," you respond, straightening up, "But really, where *isn't* that the case these days?"

All the sounds of the night—the scream of the helicopter, the scream of the monsters outside—echo inside the calm of your own mind as you lean down, picking up the last few feet of excess tether line. As some unseen, faraway winch continues to turn, you throw the coils of thick, prickly rope out the attic window.

This will either work or it won't, you think, as you step onto the windowsill, and feel the downward breeze of the helicopter as it churns the air. For a moment, you're aware of movement from every direction: the dry, jagged branches trembling in the downdraft, the orange glow of fires just a few streets away, the million clambering zombies on your lawn, biting and tearing at everything and nothing.

You look down, assessing the length of the tether line as it runs down into darkness, and then back up to the copter. *If I can just fall far enough to be past the branches,* you think, *it won't matter if I swing toward the tree. At worst, I hit the trunk, and then I swing back out.*

And dangle there while those things eviscerate us, your brain says.

"Not if they keep hauling up the rope," you say in a quiet voice.

You check once more that your body is *inside* the loose, rope-basket harness, your legs going through the netting and out the bottom.

They're going to leave, your brain says, panic creeping in.

You jump straight out, into the night air. As you plunge, it feels as though your insides are trying to burst from your mouth. For a split second, all you hear is a shrieking-kettle sound—the wind, you think—and then you run out of slack.

The tether line snaps taut with a loud, frightening *bang*—jerking you back upward; it feels as though your bones are coming apart at the joints.

The harness swings in wild arcs, like an overzealous wrecking ball, but manages to avoid actually hitting the oak tree, so far as you can tell.

You're afraid you've broken the ropes, that you'll be on the ground, helpless, while those things crawl all over you. This is replaced almost instantly by a radiating, electric pain that fills the corners of your body, seeming to roll from one set of nerves to another, like waves rocking a ship.

Eventually, the motion of the harness slows. You open your eyes and find yourself swaying, moving back and forth like a spent, un-spooled yo-yo. The harness seems intact, though it feels like you've broken everything else.

Looking straight up, you see a distant, tiny square of light: the open hatchway of a helicopter—distant, but directly above you. Somewhere inside, a winch is turning, bringing up the tether line, lifting you to safety.

The pain is such that you have difficulty looking down; you have no way to figure out how far above the ground you are.

The next few minutes are the most terrifying of your life. As the harness lifts, inch by inch, moment by excruciating moment, you wait for the agonizing tear of claws or teeth; for something to drag you back down to earth. You hear the moans, loud and broken, wailing beneath you; several times, you feel what you're certain are the ragged, scrabbling hands of a zombie grasping at your feet, at your clothes . . . and missing . . . always just missing. Your legs ache, but you clench them as high and tight as you can.

The helicopter slowly comes into focus, its open hatchway glowing against the sky. Somewhere inside, a winch is turning, bringing in the tether line, lifting you to safety.

There is an awful, nauseating smell—the copter's blades are blowing dust, piles of garbage, and the stomach-churning aroma of rotted blood and flesh. It's sweet—like candy inside a septic tank. You close your eyes, trying to picture yourself already in the helicopter—already flying away from this stench, this noise, this hell of chaos and screaming.

Deep inside your memory, a tiny light flicks on. You open your eyes, not wanting to look . . . unable to keep from looking.

Small, pathetic, looking more like a child marionette than an actual person, the man hugging on to the chimney is staring straight at you . . . eyes wide with more fear than a human being would seem capable of creating.

An angry scream of frustration fills your throat. You have to at least *try* to do something; if you don't, those desperate, pleading eyes will be in every dream you'll ever have.

Hating every second, every instant of the motion, you lift your arm and grab the tether line. Your teeth are clenched as you yank the rope twice in rapid succession.

From the belly hatchway of the helicopter, the winch operator looks down, then turns toward the pilot. His mouth moves, but you can't hear anything above the engine's roar. The helicopter continues its ascent.

You pull hard at the tether line; the harness continues its lift.

Goddammit, you think, *I just want out of this place. I just want out.*

Now or never, your brain replies. *He'll be dead the next time they make it back here.*

As the harness scrapes against the side of your house, lifting you toward safety, you look for some way to hook yourself, to stop the upward motion. Your eyes fix on the roof's edge—jutting out past the house and curling under. You lean out with your left hand and grab the underside of the wood-and-shingle outcropping. *Get ready,* your brain says. Your grip tightens, waiting for the pain.

It doesn't take long. The helicopter's winch cranks you steadily higher, and your left arm is wrenched with a tearing sound. Pain fills the place between your shoulder and your bicep. As your damaged left arm loses its grip on the roof, the harness sways, going off kilter, sending vibrations up through the cable, into the copter. Your right hand gives another two sharp yanks on the tether line, every movement like filling your left arm with lit kerosene.

It's enough. The winch operator is looking down from the hatchway, his features becoming more distinct as the harness ascends. With one clear, exaggerated motion, you point toward the chimney.

Looking toward the cockpit, the winch man presses his helmet's microphone against his mouth; his lips form sentences you can't decipher.

You stare upward, teeth clenched, eyes watering from the gust and pain. *If they bring me up, they bring me up,* you think, *but I have to at least—*

The harness stops with a sudden *chunk,* and you are suspended, swaying in the updraft. The chopper hovers, a giant metal gull drowning you in noise and wind.

The copter's engines whine higher. It lifts slightly—and you can see for miles in every direction. Miles of smoke . . . and fire . . . and churning, writhing streets filled with the undead . . . like a bloodstream clotted with insects.

You look up at the winch man; the copter banks to the left, angling toward the clinging, desperate survivor.

As you get closer to the chimney, you're amazed that *it's* still there, let alone its sole occupant. The bricks are spiderwebbed with cracks, having suffered from decades of slow disintegration. It's also much, much smaller and narrower than it seemed from a distance.

They couldn't push it over, you think, surveying the infestation below.

Or they just didn't know how, your brain answers.

It's another ninety excruciating seconds before the copter is in position, hovering above the chimney—wind from the rotors blowing your harness back and forth.

Your damaged left arm radiates with pain. You wonder if next time, you should injure your *right* arm, just for variety.

You look up at the winch man. He stares back until he's sure he's got your attention, then he holds up an index finger and gestures hard, once: *You get one try, and then we're leaving.*

You look down at the chimney and at the frail, sad figure clinging to this brick lifeboat in an ocean of living corpses. His eyes, squinting against the dust and grit blown by the helicopter, make contact with yours. He knows this is his only chance.

As the copter's winch slowly feeds out cable, lowering you toward the chimney, you're still working out the plan. He's nearly dead from dehydration and hunger . . . too much muscle loss . . . he'll never be able to hold on to the harness, much less pull himself inside. You look at your left arm . . . broken . . . useless.

You're descending, only a few feet from the chimney.

This will not be easy.

Two feet away.

You will not give up.

Almost there.

You will not give in.

Your shoes touch the sides of the chimney.

Now or never.

Letting the rope-and-webbing structure of the harness fold into itself, you stretch out, coming to rest facedown, directly on top of the other man, mirroring his position.

Without hesitating, you slide your right arm underneath the man's chest—your fingers emerging on the other side until they find your left shirtsleeve. Grabbing a tight fistful of cloth, and giving yourself no time to reconsider, you pull your right arm back underneath, your shattered left arm being dragged along like a reluctant caboose.

The pain is beyond comprehension. You know that if you stop, you'll stop for good, so you scream, pulling harder, and somehow, when you stop screaming, your left arm is in position, as though you're performing an off-center Heimlich maneuver.

Now now now now now.

With your weight resting on the chimney, the harness is relatively slack. You grab a section of the mesh webbing and loop it around your left wrist, binding it like a handcuff. Lashed into the contraption, your injured left arm is about to function as the world's most morbid seat belt. Holding your breath, you pull on the tether line and jerk a thumbs-up to the winch man without lifting your head.

The helicopter's engines crank louder, and the machine ascends, lifting both you and your barely conscious passenger. The harness tightens under his weight, going taut, cinching your left hand into place.

Hold on. You and your brain, speaking in unison.

As you swing out from the chimney, your broken left arm receiving the full weight of this injured stranger, a reeling agony screams through your shoulder and fills your consciousness.

Blind with pain, you don't see that down below, the zombies are now more than a thousand deep as they surge toward the blinking red light in your front yard.

Your house is still standing; your doors are still intact.

EPILOGUE

THERE IS NO CURE

PROTECTING YOURSELF FROM
FUTURE THREATS

They thought you might be infected. That's why they used the rope harness. The pilot, whom you never got a chance to actually meet, had done a few "scan and grabs"—search–and–rescue flights—that went horribly wrong when a seemingly healthy survivor started attacking the lowered crewman. Other pilots had made the mistake of loading passengers into the cabin of a chopper, only to find themselves fending off a zombie five minutes later.

By the time they came for you, procedure had changed. They weren't taking any chances—even *after* you were rescued. Once departed from the chimney, the helicopter flew over acres of smoldering, ruined landscape, making its way to a military hospital near the top of a nearby mountain range.

You had passed out from pain and exhaustion and didn't see yourself being lowered into what looked like a cattle pen . . . a cattle pen with steep, angled walls and ringed with gun slots. You didn't see the orange-tipped rifle that fired a powerful sedative into your body, and the body of the delirious chimney man.

You didn't see masked, garbed figures entering the pen to handcuff and restrain you.

You weren't awake for most of the tests.

When you regain full consciousness three days later, you've been cleared of any infection. Your left arm is filled with potentially troublemaking issues: bone fragments, torn rotator cuff, trauma to your tendons, severe scarring. The chimney man's weight was enough to stop blood circulation to large sections of your forearm . . . so much for his emaciation being a help. There's talk of amputating the arm, but after several surgeries, it's encased in thick plaster, along with much of your torso. With luck and sufficient physical therapy, you'll recover.

The rest of your body fared much better: you're suffering from advanced fatigue and muscle stress, and you're covered with hundreds of nicks, scrapes, scratches, and cuts, but you're otherwise healthy.

In the most relative sense possible, your brain often remarks.

Your starched hospital bed sits inside a gigantic room. It looks like a barracks that was converted for patient use, but there are only two other people: a girl—maybe twelve—and her grandfather. They're transferred somewhere else a few days after you wake up.

You ask about your mother and sister. No one has seen them. Records show that they *did* arrive at Marshall Hospital, ten miles away, but that was only days before the fire destroyed most of that building. Evacuation was haphazard, and there's no way to know where many of the refugees ended up.

Now and then, your questions elicit a fragment of a clue: someone thinks they *might* have seen a girl who *could* have looked like that . . . *maybe.* One man—a fellow patient; muscular, middle-aged, with wiry gray hair—breaks down sobbing at the word "sister." He's still sobbing four hours later when the nurses sedate and remove him.

You scan "survivor lists"—maddeningly vague, incomplete collections of names and characteristics. Sometimes, there's no more than a nickname or the description of a tattoo . . . usually meaning the Jane or John Doe is unable to speak, or write, or remember.

You check lists from all over the city, all over the state. You rack your brain, giving the nurses and soldiers as many possible misspellings of your family name as you can conjure . . . still nothing.

You're *sure,* though. Something in you just . . . knows. They're out there, waiting.

You ask about the chimney man. "He's got a lot of work ahead of him," says the doctor, his tone implying that—all things considered—it could have been a lot worse.

That's something, you think, flexing your right hand. The scarring will be bad, but . . .

Your eyes stare at nothing for just a moment. Your hand stops in mid-flex.

I made it.

You drive the doctors crazy asking when you'll be able to leave. They aren't fooling around, though—it's apparent that you'll be in this place until they decide otherwise.

As the days and weeks tick by, you have a whole new appreciation for what "the good life" really is. Your water, run from a chlorinated tap and served in a plastic cup, is nonetheless cold and clear . . . and abundant. You take showers hot enough to redden your skin and long enough to make the ceiling drip.

The sheets of the hospital bed—thin, scratchy, military-issue—feel unimaginably luxurious in their cleanness.

A clock chimes on the far wall: five o'clock. Dinner will be brought in a few minutes—a khaki-shirted doctor taking your pulse and shining a penlight in your eyes while a full plate of hot food is placed on your bedside tray.

You look out the window across the room. From here, you can see puffs of black smoke and the occasional helicopter. Every now and again, a jet streaks across the sky. For the first time, you believe that the authorities might, in fact, be doing something.

Nothing is forever. Not feast, not famine, not a bull market, not the Zombie Economy.

For some of you, salvation is still a work in progress. There are battles to be fought, harrowing obstacles to overcome, and terrifying, destructive forces you must—and will—defeat.

For others, victory is at hand. You are emerging from the tunnel—stronger, wiser, and with a powerful new perspective on what it means to persevere. Along the way, you have refined the skills you already possessed, and you have created—from your own wits and determination—the tools you needed but did not have.

You have adapted.

You have endured.

You have overcome.

You have survived.

Now is the time to secure your future—to make certain your survival isn't a temporary fluke.

It only takes one bite to restart the plague. There is no cure, there is only prevention.

Don't be caught off-guard, and always count your ammo. The zombies don't sleep.

You've come this far. Let's make sure you never go back.

We'll keep this brief—you already know most of what we're going to say. It was your mastery of these lessons that got you through the darkest times. Your strength against the Zombie Economy is like a muscle: the more you use it, the stronger it becomes, the stronger it stays. Neglect it at your peril, because the world can turn on a dime . . . or a dollar . . . or a stock-market collapse . . . or a bank failure . . . or the loss of your job . . . or an illness that depletes your savings.

The Five Rules for Long-Term Survival

1. **Ten percent of your income goes directly into savings, period.** Off the top. Before you pay one other expense. Your savings goal must be—at minimum—three months' worth of living costs, and ideally six or more. Always maintain the proper perspective: *saving is not a burden.* What saving does is *free* you—from stress, from worry, from the iron grip of other people's control.

2. **Pay your bills.** Pay them early, pay them often. For ongoing, fixed-cost necessities (rent, power, insurance), set up online bill paying or an autopay system. Set a monthly (or biweekly) date for dealing with the rest, and stay on schedule. While no one enjoys getting rid of money, the sense of relief that accompanies "cleaning the slate" never loses its power.

3. **Set, achieve, and reset your goals.** Aim for three months' savings in the bank. Then six.

   Want to buy a house? Want to avoid having that house taken away in four years? Commit to putting 20 percent down.

Want to make it through old age without eating canary food? Decide to put $150 per month into some kind of investment.

Remember: If you don't set (and reestablish) financial goals, you are far more likely to find yourself veering off course.

4. **Keep your records; check your records.**

If you're not tracking your own behavior, it's easy to spend more than you anticipate . . . and more than you realize. This doesn't mean balancing your checkbook every single day, nor does it mean that you must become some kind of walking OCD exhibit. But it does mean having a schedule/system for knowing your true income and your true expenses.

5. **Stick with the plan.** Even when you feel invincible. *Especially* when you feel invincible. Remember: The zombie threat is never gone.

Life is meant to be lived, and savored, and enjoyed . . . so make sure that you don't undermine yourself with destructive behavior. Budget for holidays, for vacations, for big purchases . . . and for frivolity. Set aside money that has no particular purpose.

Through all of this, keep in mind: spending does not bring happiness. If you ever doubt that fact, think back to your previous financial woes. Pay a visit to a credit counseling center. Spend the evening in the presence of a debt-ridden couple.

Prepare. Prevent. Persevere.

Because there is no cure.

All You Really Need to Know, You Learned in the Zombie Apocalypse

1. **Be alert to signs of infection.**

   In yourself: Assess your own financial tendencies—how are you most likely to slip up? What are your destructive habits? Simply being aware of your own personal danger spots is a massive step toward avoiding them. Be brutally honest about your patterns; if you don't identify them, the Zombie Economy will do it for you.

   In others: Your friends, family, and loved ones all have—or possess the potential to have—a disproportionate influence on your behavior, in ways both good and bad. While it's admirable to be a positive example, you *must* recognize the destructive habits of others, especially when they pose a danger to your well-being.

In the world: Actions have effects, and plagues have beginnings. Your company, your community, your country, your planet—all of these are intricate, interconnected financial systems, operating at levels of complexity that, sometimes, can barely be comprehended.

This does not, however, mean abandoning any attempt to monitor their actions and status. Self-preservation means self-education. Learn how to spot the indicators that point toward trouble.

2. **Set limits . . . and keep them.** Just as the epidemic might announce itself with a cough or a fever, your financial backslide can come without fanfare, and with only minor warning signs. To recognize these symptoms for what they are, you will need parameters on your own financial conduct.

Whether it's the number of lattes you buy per week, the amount you spend on brand-new books, or the money you're prepared to lose in a poker game, create boundaries on your purchasing and consumption habits.

Once those boundaries are in place, they must become an internalized part of your behavior: "three hardcovers a month" *means just that*. Don't accept weakness from yourself, and do not shrug your lapses away, as so many others do. *You are better than that*; you are made of sterner stuff.

When you fail to stay within your limits, accept it, but ask yourself *how* it happened, and how it can be avoided in the future. Keeping (and checking) basic financial records

will alert you to signs that you might be resuming old
behaviors.

Let's be clear: We're all for fun. We're fun incarnate. We're
talking about following rules and respecting boundaries
that you have set for yourself.

Identifying your own areas of economic risk does no
good if you repeatedly return there.

3. **Keep the pain of debt firmly in mind.** As your fiscal stability
   increases, and your income rises, it's inevitable that some of
   your spending outlays will become larger. As these numbers
   escalate, however, you need to remember that debt is debt
   is debt. A thousand dollars owed is the same thousand dollars,
   regardless of your income. Don't let a larger salary (or a
   seemingly stable job) blind you to the importance of staying
   in the black.

   Give yourself reminders: in your checkbook (or in your
   home office, or in the computer folder where you keep your
   financial info), post a note so big you can't miss it: "I owe
   (person's name) X dollars." The accruing of debt is, at times,
   unavoidable. The *paying off* of debt is always exhilarating,
   always good for your financial health, and always the right
   thing to do.

> Remember: Debt is a rusting hinge. Debt is a broken window. Debt is how they get in.

4. **You've learned to handle adversity—now make sure to handle your prosperity.** There's a certain horrible clarity that comes with facing financial doom: when your life is on the line, decisions are much easier. When you have no money for luxuries or frivolities, turning them down isn't such a chore. When you're working to keep the lights on, assessing investment options doesn't even cross your mind.

When you've made it out of the chaos, though, you'll start to see your options expanding. You'll have choices and alternatives—and responsibilities—that simply don't exist for those on the brink. We've listed some areas of special concern below.*

Taxes

Pay them. Pay them correctly. Do not end up owing the government more than you possess.

Investing

Turning ten dollars into a hundred? Difficult. Turning a thousand dollars into ten thousand? Much easier.

In this area, like most others, we remind you: seek the advice of an expert. Don't know where to start? Ask your bank.

Retirement

It's a fact that, for most people, earning power (and the ability to work) decreases as age increases.

---

* We urge you to seek the assistance and advice of professionals. This needn't be costly; many community business organizations are staffed by active or retired business leaders who can address your concerns, and/or point you toward experts in the field. (For more information on community business groups in your area, visit ZombieEconomics.com.)

Nightmare scenario: realizing you *must* keep working as you pass into your sixties and beyond.

Even worse: realizing you must work even harder than before, while earning less. Ask your bank or investment expert about planning for retirement. Don't wait: every year that you postpone the start of your retirement plan raises the odds that you will be working a dead-end, depressing job at the age of seventy.

As your worth increases, it needs just as much protection . . . but in different ways. Educate yourself, and use the services of an expert when necessary, because the Zombie Economy is always looking for new ways to attack.

5. **Beware of survivor guilt.** After a physical crisis or tragedy (a plane crash, car accident, violent crime, etc.), it is not uncommon for those who escaped unscathed (or who suffered significantly less harm/injury) to feel an overwhelming, often crippling, sense of shame or guilt. This can manifest itself in harmful or self-destructive behaviors, externalizations of the survivor's belief that they did not "deserve" to be spared, or that they are somehow betraying those who suffered worse fates.

This scenario can also occur in situations of financial crisis. As those around you—or those elsewhere in society— follow their own path to stability, they will encounter pitfalls, shortcuts, and moments of great decision. Some will prosper, perhaps fantastically so. Others will stumble, learning from their missteps and ultimately emerging as wiser, more resilient versions of themselves. And some will never attain even the smallest degree of financial success, their lives a series of bad breaks and poor choices.

This is not your fault. Whatever anyone says, no matter what any social, political, or moral institution would have you believe, this is not your fault.

You are not to feel guilt for your prosperity. Your choices, your preparation and self-discipline (and, yes, your luck), are *yours* . . . and yours alone.

Understand: We are not, under any circumstances, suggesting that you be insensitive or unsympathetic, or that you avoid helping those who are less fortunate.

What we are saying is this: A dead hero never rescued anyone.

If you are to help others, you must save yourself. It is your responsibility. Part of that responsibility takes the form of this realization:

Money is neither good nor bad; it is neither hero nor villain. Money is a tool . . . one key on a ring that holds dozens. Education, willpower, integrity, experience, the support of friends and loved ones, imagination . . . every one of them a key. All of them crucial, all of them different.

Money, like the rest, can unlock otherwise impassable doors. Without it, life becomes much harder—for you, and for those in your care.

Viewing your money—or money, period—as an object of worship or fear is to view it through a lens of counterproductive superstition. Money is a tool, a resource—no different from food, soil, or steel. It's how and where you use it that matters.

Just as important as your actions, your attitudes and outlook will play a vital role in keeping you alive. Be vigilant, be alert, be honest with yourself and others. The Zombie Economy is always searching for a weak spot—don't provide one.

6. **Most of all, remember what you went through.** You faced a powerful foe and, from time to time, may have doubted that you would emerge, victorious. *You did not yield,* however. You did not give up. You did not give in.

You persevered.

You fought.

You struggled.

You survived.

I *survived,* you think.

You're standing in front of the large hospital-room window, looking out at the ruined city. Your right arm itches from the IV drip and the antibiotics; your left arm swelters inside the lighter, thinner cast you got two weeks ago.

They pump you full of something yellow and cold twice each day; they swab your mouth and put the cotton-tipped stick into a red plastic case.

As your arm continues to mend, you focus on the exercise you *can* do: you walk the perimeter of the hospital, over and over, dozens of times a day.

Your breathing—a little on the raspy, ragged side when you got here, likely from prolonged exposure to gasoline fumes and smoke—becomes less labored.

Nine weeks after your arrival, the cast is removed from your arm. You decide to welcome it back by brushing your teeth left-handed. After twenty-five minutes, your arm feels as though it's been dipped in kerosene, and sweat is running into your eyes. You hobble back to your bed, exhausted, angry, impatient.

The next morning, you try again. You manage to get your front teeth and a couple of molars before your strength gives out.

Just another few days, says your brain that evening, as you apply toothpaste to the brush, *and you'll be ready for needle-point.*

You mangle a wet "Shut up" around a mouthful of bristles, and continue brushing, a large smile on your face.

Over time, your arm's muscles turn from agonized to merely aching. Then stiff, then sore, then something not quite bad and not quite pleasant. They're getting stronger. You ask for weights. When they don't appear, you ask for books . . . whatever they have.

You read, you lift, you recover.

You ask to see a nutritionist. "Why," they ask, "is something wrong?"

"No," you reply, shaking your head, "I'd just like it to stay that way."

As the days and weeks wear on, the news from the outside is more detailed. Though they've turned the tide against the undead, military leaders are saying it will be a long haul before things are "safe," and it might be decades before they're anything like they used to be.

You learn that your neighborhood has been classed as "B3" on the threat scale. The "B" indicates that zombies are still found in the area, though in a substantially decomposed state; "3" means they typically appear in clusters of three or fewer.

An "A" rating comes when a region is completely "clean": no zombie sightings of any kind for a minimum of six months.

There are no "A" ratings anywhere.

On the day you're released, you're given a badge with your name and picture on it, along with directions to a clinic near your home. They say that you should go to the clinic if you start to feel dizzy, or if you have any other flu-like symptoms. They also tell you that a medical survey team will be conducting weekly follow-up tests; you are to be at your home, alone, every Monday at two p.m. You'll be giving blood and saliva samples, they say.

You nod and, squinting against the sun, walk out into a cold, clear day.

Opting against taking the military shuttle, you walk down the sloping road, making sure your ID tag is visible as you wind toward the bottom of the hill. There, you're inspected for signs of illness or infection, searched, and then allowed onto a dark green bus. There are armed guards stationed at the front and back.

Looking out the window as the bus rolls toward the city, you see fortifications everywhere: heavy fencing, motion sensors, foot patrols. The ground forces—like the sentries on this bus—wear a "bleeder": a bodysuit made of lightweight polymer. Between the suit's two layers is a fluorescent dye. Get bitten or clawed—hell, *shot*—and there's no hiding it. Not anymore.

For the hundredth time that day, you take out your notebook and study the list of hospitals that fall within fifty miles—the ones still standing, anyway. Some are accessible, some are quarantined, and a few are still so deep inside hot zones that no one knows when— or if—they'll ever be fully searched.

Forty-five minutes later, the bus arrives in the center of downtown. Passengers are searched as they depart. The bus is cleaned, sprayed, and rechecked while another group waits to board.

As you pass by empty housing lots, empty business lots, and empty acres of blocked-off nothing, you know that most of what you stockpiled at home will be gone. Not from looters, but from the military—as the government fought their way through the city, inch by inch, house by house, they took refuge inside homes like yours, using what was there, taking what they needed.

You know you'll need to rebuild. You know you'll need to prepare all over again.

Something glints on the ground. You bend down and pick it up.

A single bullet.

Tucking it into your pocket, you keep walking, keep moving forward.

THE END

ACKNOWLEDGMENTS

Due to luck or fate, many people with brilliance and patience blessed this book with their support.

Understand that we may accidentally leave someone out, but we must express our deepest gratitude to those who helped *Zombie Economics* come to life and take its first breath.

Maestro Peter Carlin kindly did not laugh when presented with the "demo" version of the book, and was beyond generous with his knowledge.

Supercorpse Todd Werkhoven contributed an equal mix of horrific imagery and practical structure . . . all while maintaining his gig as a Sunday-school teacher and leader of church music.

Particularly deep thanks go to the fearless, tireless Cheryl Kanekoa, without whom this book likely would be in limbo. If the apocalypse comes, you want her on your anti-brute squad.

Rodger Bridges, artist nonpareil, created designs that turned imagination into reality . . . in more ways than one.

Our agent, Dan Conaway, effortlessly steered us though daunting, unfamiliar waters like a Jedi. Señor Conaway told us early on, "Wow, you guys aren't fucking around," which is certain to be one of the best compliments the book receives. Publication of this book is also thanks to Stephen Barr, his assistant, and an important part of the zombie crew.

Editor Rachel Holtzman at Avery brought *Zombie Economics* into focus and strengthened our theme and idea. Rachel was wonderful and tolerated the twitchy, obsessive behavior of two neurotic writers with remarkable aplomb and humor.

Our very first reader, Trevor Farrell, and Serena Werkhoven, Robert Bennett, Sigfried Seeliger, Tim Oakley, Dan Haneckow, and Storm Large all contributed intelligence, honesty, and charm. Sarah X. Dylan, Greg Nibler, Tim Riley, and Bruce Agler gave us critical early support and encouragement superb. Our lawyers, Kohel Haver (Swider Medeiros Haver LLP) and Owen Dukelow (Kolisch Hartwell, P.C.), provided advice, acumen, and legal power.

Lee Banville served as friend and a key adviser to Zombie Economics.com, and is responsible for setting up our backup escape cabin in Montana.

Special thanks go to CNN Radio, the DC3, the Capitol Hill unit, and managers Tyler Moody and Dan Szematowicz for their constant support, inspiration, and Bob's fettuccine.

Other thanks to:

Hank, Karen, Becca, Charlie, and Marcy: a fictional family who filled a very real need in our plan.

The College of William & Mary economics department and the state of Virginia.

Offspring, whose album *Rise and Fall, Rage and Grace* was the de facto sound track to this book's creation.

President Andrew Jackson, who was the only U.S. president to see the national debt paid off, and President Chester Arthur, who defied all expectations.

Finally, we are in debt to William Strunk, E. B. White, Stephen King, and Joe Eszterhas: four men whose books on writing were invaluable.

REFERENCES

CHAPTER 4. DON'T GO IN THE GRAVEYARD

Chandra, Shobhana. "Jobless Wait a Record 34.4 Weeks for Employment." *Bloomberg*, June 2010 (citing Labor Department report).

CHAPTER 5. THEY'LL EAT THE FAT ONES FIRST

Centers for Disease Control. "Chronic Disease Prevention and Health Promotion." May 2010.

———. "Heart Disease and Stroke Prevention," 2010.

Dall, Timothy, Yiduo Zhang, and Yaozhu Chen. "The Economic Burden of Diabetes." *Health Affairs*, January 2010.

Gordon, Serena. "Men Who Smoke Prone to Impotence." *U.S. News & World Report*, December 2007.

Harvard School of Public Health. "Type-2 Diabetes." American Diabetes Association, 2007 report.

Kastner, Mike. "What Will Health Care Reform Mean to You?" *Insurance News*, June 2010.

Mayo Clinic. "Type-2 Diabetes: Risk Factors," June 2009.

McGinnis, J. M. "Diabetes and Physical Activity: Translating Evidence into Action." *American Journal of Preventive Medicine*, 2002.

Sacks, Frank M., et al. "Comparison of Weight-Loss Diets with Different

Compositions of Fat, Protein, and Carbohydrates." *New England Journal of Medicine,* February 2009.

United Healthcare. "America's Health Rankings," November 2009.

CHAPTER 6. SURVIVING THE GRAVEYARD

Rosenthal, Dave. "Reading Is Good for Your Health." *Baltimore Sun,* April 13, 2009 (citing 2009 University of Sussex report).

INDEX

Better Business Bureaus, 189
Bills, 7–12
  assessing, 10
  medical, 5, 52, 91, 206, 212–13
  recurring, 167–68
  worksheet for credit card bills,
    42–43
  as zombies, 10
Biohazard icon, 6
Blaming the victim, 135
Books, borrowing from library, 40
Borrowing
  v. buying, 230
  nonemergency, 149
Bounced checks, 172–73
Brain food icon, 6
Bureau of Labor Statistics, 124
Business research, on Internet, 189
Buying *v.* borrowing, 230

Cable television, 36, 39, 45, 128
Calculator, for withholding, 30
Calendars, 45, 119, 131, 245
Calorie reduction, 98
Canceling, credit cards, 184*n*
Cancer self-screenings, 100–101
Career-building potential, 125
Car payments, 4, 33, 213
Carrying credit cards, 169–70
Cars
  lending, 151
  repossession of, 4, 53, 154, 157*n*
Cashier's checks, 188
Cell phone plans, 39, 53, 128,
  150, 152
Check-cashing services, 148
Checks, bounced, 172–73
Child support, 12*n*, 33, 211
Chronic diseases, 91*n*
  and bankruptcy, 91
  heart disease, 94–95
  lung disease, 95
  preventable, 90–92, 95
  type 2 diabetes, 92–94
Cigarettes, 37, 91, 95, 130
Clearance sales, 183

Closeout sales, 183
Cohabitating, with financial
  "zombies," 153
Collateral, 150, 152
College financing, 188
Commission fees, 184
Compounded interest, 54–55, 54*n*
Compulsive spending, 156
Consolidation, of debt, and
  bankruptcy, 187
Cosigning loans, 150, 152
Counseling centers, 134, 261
Counterfeit forms of payment,
  188
Craigslist, 129
Credit card(s)
  annual fees on, 183–84
  canceling, 184*n*
  carrying, 169–70
  credit scores and, 184*n*
  debt, 4–5, 41–43, 56
  minimum payments on, 31, 33, 41,
    43–44
  offers, 11
  overview of, 41–42
  from stores, 183
  worksheet for credit card bills,
    42–43
Credit counseling, 209
Credit reports, 203, 205
Credit scores, 93, 224, 228
  credit cards and, 184*n*
  debt and, 150
  definition of, 150*n*
  restoration of, 188
  of spouse, 152
Cross-border bankruptcy, 203

Death wish, 135*n*
Debit cards, 168, 172–73, 229*n*
Debt(s), 10, 18
  credit card, 4–5, 41–43, 56
  credit scores and, 150
  debt consolidation, 187
  freedom from, 58
  pain of, 263

Money (*cont.*)
  asking parents for, 77
  as a tool, 266
Money orders, 188
Monthly average, of absolute
    necessities, 60
Monthly goals of spending, 36–38
Monthly income, average, 22–23, 27
Monthly "leaks," 38, 285
Monthly operating fund, 32–34,
    226, 285
Monthly reminders, 45
Mortgages, 31–32, 52, 187, 213
  mortgage anxiety, 187
Motivation, 18, 75–76
  education and, 57
  exercise and, 133
  external, 170
Movie subscription services, 39–40, 45
Movie/video game rentals, 36,
    39–40, 128
Moving in, with parents, 53
Municipal bankruptcy, 202
Myths, about bankruptcy, 205–6

National recessions, 4
Necessities, absolute, 11–12, 31–34,
    229, 285
  monthly average of, 60
Nonemergency borrowing, 149
Nonworking spouse, 29
"No Risk" schemes, 185

Obesity, 93, 95
Obsessive-compulsive behavior,
    62, 260
Occupational employment and wage
    estimates, 124
Occupational Employment Statistics,
    124
Odd jobs, 25
Offers
  for credit cards, 11
  limited-time, 182
Online. *See also* Internet
  applying for unemployment, 229n

banking, 58
communities, 172n
job sites, 124
payments, 12, 259
tools, 230
worksheets, 225
Operating fund, monthly, 32–34,
    226, 285
Opportunities, for advancement, 70
Outstanding loans, 4
Overage penalties, 172
Overdrafts, disallowing, 172–73
Overpayment, of tax, 20, 28
Overseas labor, 69
Overspending, 148–49, 154, 169

Pain, of debt, 263
Parents
  asking for money from, 77
  elderly, 30
  moving in with, 53
  as zombies, 153–54
Password, for ZombieEconomics
    .com, 225
Pawning, your television, 68
Paychecks
  as ammunition, 126
  average, 21–22
Payday-advances, 148
Paying off debt, 263
Paying yourself, 53–54
Payment plans, 202, 209
Payments
  online, 12, 259
  of tax, 12n, 212, 264
Penalty fees, 41, 43, 152–53, 167, 172
Personal economy, 5, 5n, 90, 224
Personal responsibility, 170–72, 223
Phone, 32, 39, 53, 128, 150, 152.
    See also Cell phone plans
Predators, financial, 177–93
Predatory lenders, 143n
Preventable chronic diseases,
    90–92, 95
Primary income, 21, 61
Principal amount, 54n

W-4 tax form, 29–31
Wage estimates, 124
Walking, 129
Warehouse clubs, 40
Water, 221–22
  bottled, 101
  tap, 256
"Weak spots," financial, 18, 35–36
Web page design, 230
Website(s)
  state government–sponsored, 229n
  subscriptions for, 38
  for workforce/unemployment, 127
Weekly reminders, 45
Wellness programs, 91
Withholding
  calculator for, 30
  tax, 28, 28n
  worksheet for, 29–31
Workforce/unemployment
      websites, 127
Workout maximization, 94
Work-related stress, 74
Worksheets
  for absolute necessities and
      operating fund, 32–34
  for bankruptcy, 212–13
  for credit card bills, 42–43
  for emergency savings, 60–61
  for finding fulfillment outside of
      work, 75–76
  for income, 21
  for income summary, 27
  for job change, 70–71
  for key survival numbers, 285
  for magic number, 226–27
  online, 225

for other income, 25–26
for spending, 36–39
for tips, 23–24
for tracking job search, 119–20
for withholding, 29–31
Work space, 10–11

Yard sales, 129
Yearly reminders, 45

Zero tolerance, of financial
      irresponsibility, 154
Zombie apocalypse, ix, 92, 186
  learning from, 231, 261
  surviving, 6, 126
Zombie bait, 156n
Zombie Economics
  bankruptcy and, 202–11
  definition of, ix
ZombieEconomics.com, 24, 168n
  password for, 225
Zombie Economist, 54, 54n
Zombie Economy
  definition of, 4–5
  outlasting, 25, 58, 258
  victims of, 155, 181
Zombies, 1
  avoiding, 6, 16
  bills as, 10
  cohabitating with, 153
  curing, 154–55
  ending relationships with, 143–61
  killing, 11, 44
  loans as, 10
  parents as, 153–54
  "zombie" spouses, 151n

FINAL WORKSHEET: KEY SURVIVAL NUMBERS

Monthly Income: _____

Worksheet #4, page 27

Absolute Necessities Cost: _____

Worksheet #6, page 34

Monthly Operating Fund: _____

Worksheet #6, page 34

Potential Monthly Leaks:

Worksheet #7, page 38

_____ (month 1)

_____ (month 2)

_____ (month 3)

_____ (month 4)

_____ (month 5)

_____ (month 6)

Emergency Savings Goal:

Worksheet #9, page 60

Total amount _____

How Many Months of Expenses? _____